WHY ON EARTH

Distributed by

Gifts of the Spirit Church

and Psychic Research Center

1595 Route 85

Chesterfield, Connecticut 06370

(203) 443-3201

Why on Earth

An Introduction to the
Ancient Wisdom through
White Eagle's teaching

Joan Hodgson

The White Eagle Publishing Trust
Liss . Hampshire . England
1982

First published as Why on Earth: the
Light of the Ancient Wisdom on Modern
Problems, *under the name Joan Cooke,*
    October 1964
First paperback edition,
entirely revised, enlarged and reset
    September 1979
Reprinted
    July 1982

British Library Cataloguing
in Publication Data
Hodgson, Joan
    Why on earth.—[New ed.].
    1. White Eagle Lodge
    2. Spiritualism—Great Britain
    133.9   BF1283.W/

    ISBN 0-85487-043-1

Set in 11 on 13 pt Monophoto Baskerville
by Richard Clay (The Chaucer Press) Ltd
and printed in Great Britain by
Fletcher & Son Ltd, Norwich

Contents

The writer of this book expresses her thanks to all who have helped in its compilation; and above all her gratitude to White Eagle and those helpers gathered with him, upon whose inspiration, teaching and practical wisdom such a restatement as this necessarily depends.

Publisher's Preface (1979)

Joan Hodgson first wrote *Why on Earth* for publication in 1964 in response to many requests, particularly from young people in the White Eagle Lodge, for a book which would explain in the most basic terms the teachings of the Ancient Wisdom, as given by White Eagle. The present edition is a larger book, substantially revised. Chapter 1 has been expanded to include a discussion of the use and abuse of hallucinatory drugs, and the section on karma in chapter 4 has been reorganised. Chapter 6 now describes the technique of yoga- or God-breathing, and the passages in chapter 9 on the projection of the Christ Star have been expanded. Chapter 8 has been completely rewritten.

In the new matter quotations from two books have been made, and we are grateful to their publishers for permission to do so: to Radha Soami Satsang Beas (Punjab, India), for the passage from *Liberation of the Soul* by J. Stanley White; and to A. Thomas & Co. for the passage from Indra Devi's *Forever Young, Forever Healthy*.

Introduction

The modern world appears confused and beset with problems which affect all who walk life's path. Although such problems have always existed, they are now made more complex by the increasing speed and freedom of modern life, and are vividly brought home to everyone through television, radio and the press. At the same time, man's attachment to science and technology seems gradually to be destroying alike both superstition and conventional religion, depriving many people of the faith which sustained their forefathers and yet failing to offer in its place the guiding star which deep in their hearts, even if unconsciously, people long for.

Is it possible, in the face of the apparent destruction of religious faith, to discern a constant star by which men may guide their lives? Is it possible to uncover a science of religion revealing eternal spiritual laws, which do not change as dogmas pass away, and which govern human evolution as surely as the visible universe is governed by the laws of physics? In

1

this book I have tried to introduce the reader to the religious teaching known as the Ancient Wisdom. This Wisdom, which is older than man himself, is the basis of all the world's religions, and has always been available to the man who searches. Before the time of Jesus, its light was kept burning and protected by brotherhoods such as the Essenes, and throughout the two thousand years since his incarnation it has been carefully watched over, that it may guide men throughout their destiny. Now, as the New Age of Aquarius opens, man is being prepared to receive the light of the Ancient Wisdom as a fund of knowledge of the purpose of his life on earth.

During the last half-century there has been a resurgence of interest in such matters as extra-sensory perception, space phenomena, spiritual healing, thought-power, and astrology. Books have been written about life after death, giving such a mass of evidence to prove man's survival, that there is no need for any sincere enquirer to remain in doubt or ignorance. Recent experiments with subjects under hypnosis have given considerable proof of man's pre-existence and reincarnation; ideas which have been accepted for centuries by the religions of the East, but are unfamiliar to orthodox Christians of the West. The truth of astrology, too, is easily demonstrable to anybody who is prepared to gain sufficient knowledge to set up his own birth chart and study its implications. The findings of some among the world's most eminent scientists and psychologists suggest a plan of events and the existence of a power behind all manifested life which is beyond the comprehension of the most brilliant intellect. In the light of the proof available to the impartial student, there can no longer be any excuse for failing to come to terms with the new knowledge available to man.

During the latter part of the nineteenth century three movements came into being whose work was to give to the Western world a spiritual understanding which could keep pace with the growth of material science, and meet its searching analysis in a way impossible with the blind faith of Christian orthodoxy. These three movements were Modern Spiritualism, Christian Science and Theosophy. Spiritualism sprang from the psychic phenomena spontaneously demonstrated to the Fox sisters in the United States. Christian Science, or the science of creative thought, was developed through the work of Mary Baker Eddy and P. P. Quimby. Theosophy (and its important variation Anthroposophy, developed by Rudolf Steiner) began with Madame Blavatsky's study of the occult

3

and her subsequent writings. Each of these movements expounded spiritual law in a way suited to different types of mentality.

Of the three, Spiritualism particularly has given abundant and tangible proof to the Western world of man's survival after physical death. The psychic phenomena produced during the earlier days of Spiritualism were amazingly evidential and brought into the movement such eminent thinkers as Sir Oliver Lodge, Sir William Crookes, Sir Arthur Conan Doyle and W. T. Stead. Gifted natural mediums have proved to millions of people that the soul survives death and can communicate with those still in the flesh.

At first much of this mediumship was of a physical nature, producing the materialised form or voice of the communicator, or demonstrating the existence of a super-physical power (such as is also possessed by some yogis in the East).

Gradually, however, 'physical phenomena' as these manifestations were called—gave place to a subtler form of mediumship, in which the medium became over-shadowed or entranced by a different personality known as the guide, who used the physical brain and voice of the medium rather as an instrument through which to project, to those still in the physical

4

body, tidings of friends living in the state of being which follows death. Among these, a few great names stood out, and notably that of White Eagle, a name for 'the wise teacher'. Through his medium, Mrs Grace Cooke, White Eagle has not only given convincing proof of survival to hundreds of enquirers, but began about 1930 to unfold a philosophy which, he said, was a restatement of the Ancient Wisdom. These teachings, combined with the most convincing proofs of spiritual guidance and care were given first in a circle which included Mrs Cooke's family and a small group of helpers, and then to an ever-widening public.

White Eagle states that he is one of a band of workers in the inner or soul-world, known as the White Brotherhood, or more usually now the Star Brotherhood, whose work is to watch over the evolution of humanity and bring it safely through much trial and testing into a new Golden Age. Of this Brotherhood it has been said: 'There is a vast and perfectly efficient spiritual organisation for the sustenance of mankind. God has never left mankind without a witness; the truth of the Ancient Wisdom has never been allowed to fade from the knowledge of humanity. Through countless years brothers and sages have received the wisdom and have

5

been guided to the work of inspiring men and women to seek and discover, hidden in the vaults of the subconscious, the sweet and beautiful truth of the Divine Light which ever brings happiness to the soul.'

White Eagle is such a brother. The pages which follow are based wholly upon his teaching; the philosophy they outline has been tested over many decades.

White Eagle says: 'You all need help and inspiration in these times, for you are under constant strain; and you are weary, nervously, mentally, physically.

'My brethren, the one sustenance all mankind can receive is strength from God.'

Who is this God to whom White Eagle would have us turn?

In most religious teaching, confusion arises between the personal and impersonal aspects of the deity. The idea of a personal God, enthroned in a heaven above the bright blue sky, was probably well suited to the undeveloped minds of primitive races, but modern man, accustomed to the idea of space travel, needs a more adequate conception with a far wider view of the relationship of man to God and the cosmos.

White Eagle says that God, the Great Spirit, creator of worlds, is an infinite intelligence

6

quite beyond the comprehension of man's finite mind. *No man hath seen God at any time*, but the Ancient Wisdom states that God the unmanifest, the first cause, reveals himself to limited human understanding through the Cosmic Christ, that great spirit known as the Son of God, who finds embodiment, to our physical eyes, in the sun. The sun is in a sense a physical vehicle for the glorious universal presence behind it, which gives light and being to all life, and also in a mystical way permeates it, so that all creation has within it a spark of the sun, a cell of the divine, which will ultimately grow to full stature as a perfect son–daughter of God.

The growth and development of this inner light of the Christ Spirit can only take place through incarnation. Just as fire can only burn and increase when it has fuel, so the flame of the spirit only increases when infused into matter, which it slowly irradiates and transforms.

Between the pure flame of divine spirit and the cold weight of inanimate matter lie many varied states of being, of matter vibrating at separate rates. The incarnating spirit clothes itself in a number of different garments or vehicles of consciousness, each relating to these varied states, before finally coming to birth in a physical body. These intermediate vehicles are

7

counterparts of the physical body, but as they vibrate at a higher rate they are invisible to the physical eye. They are untouched by death and form the soul body which the spirit continues to use in what we may describe as the higher, or perhaps more accurately the inner, world beyond death, until it is once again ready to put on a 'coat of flesh'.

These finer vehicles which constitute the soul interpenetrate the physical body and are closely related to the nerve centres and ductless glands. They manifest as the personality by which we recognise each other.

White Eagle teaches that just as man has three aspects, body, soul and spirit, so the Great White Spirit, God the creator, is triune. Some philosophers and metaphysicians describe the three aspects as universal power, wisdom and love, but White Eagle usually simplifies the conception into the universal holy family—God the Father, the great first cause, the power-current of positivity throughout all worlds; God the Mother, similarly the wisdom-current of negativity or receptivity; and, born of the perfect balance and union of these two, Christ the Son, or, perhaps more aptly, the Son–Daughter of God, the Light of God made manifest, bringing order out of chaos, creating worlds and universes.

Since man is made 'in the image of God', he too manifests the triune qualities of power, wisdom and love. The power aspect of his nature is the positive energy, will and vitality, physical and mental which he uses in his struggle for existence. When this aspect predominates the temperament is positive or extrovert.

The wisdom aspect is the negative or receptive faculty, linked with the feelings and emotions by which man is made aware of the more subtle factors in life; when this predominates the temperament is introvert. As man evolves and gradually learns to bring these two aspects into perfect balance, the inner light which was shining in the darkness—*and the darkness comprehended it not*—begins to manifest as warm human love, which gradually evolves from a limited personal feeling to a universal compassion.

Through the development of the wisdom aspect of his nature man becomes aware of the hidden worlds beyond death. This awareness can bring great comfort in times of pain and affliction, for through it can be found a mystical comradeship with those saints and seers of all time who have trodden the same hard path towards spiritual mastery; who can therefore give their struggling younger brethren the courage and hope, as White Eagle says, 'to keep on keeping on', and the understanding which brings healing and consolation.

When Jesus spoke of the Holy Ghost, the comforter, he was referring to this wisdom aspect both in man and in the Cosmos, through which his disciples could receive heavenly counsel and consolation after his physical presence had been withdrawn from them. Wise, loving counsel, comfort and succour is the gift of motherhood throughout creation, and it is through the development of this wisdom aspect of his being that man becomes aware of the Christ-presence both within and outside himself. In mystical terms the Divine Mother aspect in man as in the Cosmos gives birth to the Light—the Christ-consciousness.

The Divine Mother is personified in all religions. Christians turn to Mary, the mother of Jesus, but orthodox teachings do not make clear the mystical truth that just as Jesus personifies the Cosmic Christ, so Mary personifies the universal mother aspect of God, and Joseph the father aspect.

Because the family unit on earth is a personification of this universal Holy Trinity and is ideally its counterpart, the family is one of the most powerful factors for good or ill in all human experience.

1. The Precession of the Equinoxes and the Cycle of Evolution

When, faced with sorrow or calamity, people say 'How can a God of love allow such things to happen?' they do not understand how God, creator of universes, brought into being at their creation laws of evolution which are in every detail just, perfect and true. The ancient axiom, 'As above, so below; as in heaven, so on earth', reflects how both physical and spiritual laws are demonstrated in the natural rhythms of the tides, the days and the seasons, and in the celestial rhythms of planets and constellations. Indeed, the stars in their courses not only demonstrate the physical laws of the universe, but in a mysterious way set the rhythms that govern the circumstances of men.

Let us dwell on this for a moment. Astronomers know that over a period of roughly 26,000 years the relationship of the earth to the sun slowly alters, in a process known as the precession of the equinoxes. The position of the

11

sun at the spring equinox on earth (known as the vernal point) alters in relation to the constellations, gradually receding through the twelve signs of the zodiac and passing into a different constellation about every two thousand years. These two-thousand-year periods are known as Ages, the twelve of them forming a complete cycle. They are the months of the Great Year.

Historic and prehistoric records reveal that as the vernal point nears the cusp of a zodiacal sign, the imaginary line marking the division between one sign and the next, humanity passes through a difficult transition during which the old order decays and gives place to a new one. This period is usually marked by social upheavals and frequent outbreaks of war. There is a time of apparent moral decadence, during which the outworn forms of religious observance crumble. But during this period great teachers are born in different parts of the world who give their followers a restatement of the eternal truth known as the Ancient Wisdom. The form of this restatement always corresponds with the inner significance of that constellation which the vernal point is about to enter. For instance, when the vernal point was in the constellation of Taurus, the bull was worshipped as the symbol of the deity in

12

Egypt, Crete, Babylon, Assyria and throughout the Middle East, while Britain was known as the Sacred Island of the White Bull. Astrologically, Taurus is the sign of the builder, which shows in so many of the superb Egyptian temples and monuments then erected. The bodies of important people were preserved and mummified, as the religion of that Age attached great importance to physical form.

Much of the Jewish history which forms the Old Testament took place during the following Age of Aries, a fire sign which inspired a vigorous reaction to the influence of Taurus; and the religious observances of this Age made much of burnt offerings sacrificed to the one true God.

Astrological research leads us to believe that the mid-way point in the 26,000-year cycle of the Great Year occurs at the end of the Age of Aries, or the beginning of the Age of Pisces.* At this time there comes to the earth a special outpouring of spiritual light and power which may be likened to a baptism, so that the whole consciousness of humanity is stirred and quickened. Although the effects are slow to be felt,

* Because the vernal point recedes through the constellation, the Ages, or 'months' of the Great Year, follow in reverse order to that of the Sun through the signs of the zodiac in our little year.

man's evolution takes a new turn. After this baptism, he becomes more conscious of the needs of others. His mind is stimulated to make scientific discoveries which steadily widen his horizons and urge him to learn more of the mysteries of both the material and spiritual universe, and so gain wisdom which helps him in his struggle to create a more perfect civilisation.

Astrologers believe that in the present cycle this baptism culminated in the ministry and crucifixion of Jesus of Nazareth. During the period of increased spiritual outpouring which led up to this, a number of world teachers such as Zoroaster, Gautama Buddha, Confucius and Lao Tse, were born. Each of them was in his degree a vehicle for that radiant eternal light which we will call the Cosmic Christ. Each gave for his own race a restatement of the Ancient Wisdom, the jewel of truth within the mass of dogma and superstition which always grows up around it as an Age proceeds.

The early Christians used the symbol of the fish in their religious observances. It can be seen inscribed on the walls of the catacombs as their sign. Many of the miracles of Jesus were concerned with water or with fishes; baptism by water plays an important part in the religious symbolism of Christianity, showing its affinity with the Piscean Age then dawning. The constant references in the New Testament to the 'Lamb of God which taketh away the sins of the world' bear witness to the influence of the Age of Aries which was then waning, an Age when the sacrifice of a lamb formed part of the religious observance.

Pisces is a water sign which influences the emotions. The religion of this, the Piscean Age has appealed to the emotions rather than to the mind, and has to a large extent been based on faith rather than knowledge. The religious mystics withdrew from the world and, through almost fanatical self-denial and discipline, reached a state of spiritual illumination which enabled them to inspire others with something of their own faith and vision. Apart from these illumined leaders, the Piscean Age has in many ways been one of darkness and confusion, in which different religious doctrines have been enforced with much cruelty.

We are now drawing near to the end of the Piscean Age and for some decades humanity has been responding more and more to the stimulation of the next zodiacal sign—Aquarius.

Aquarius is a sign of the air element, which stimulates the mind rather than the emotions. Perhaps the first stirrings of the new age were felt at about the same time as the discovery in

1781 of the planet Uranus, which has a strong affinity with Aquarius. Soon after this came the French Revolution, and in England the further development of the Industrial Revolution, followed by social revolutions and uprisings throughout Europe.

The strong mental stimulation of the approaching Aquarian Age has led to the rapid development of scientific knowledge and discovery; it has also given impetus to the education of the masses all over the world. Two world wars have been followed by tremendous social changes and upheavals. Just as human bodies and all natural forms develop according to their set pattern, and having reached their peak gradually disintegrate to make way for fresh growth, so customs and thought-patterns which have been built up during one Age come to the point where having lost their usefulness they must be discarded. The outpouring of the spirit of the New Age inevitably brings chaos and disruption, as the old ideas and set patterns crumble before the new are formed.

The whole of this century has been under the pressure of the incoming force, the spirit of the new age, and humanity has been passing through what the teachers in the world of spirit have called 'the years of fire'. Back in the 1930s White Eagle told his group that the later de-

16

cades of this century would bring tremendous changes in the outlook of humanity and that a much more spiritual conception of life was coming. At the time it was difficult to see how this could be. Those who worked in spiritual organisations during the 1930s had a real battle to convince people of the truths of life after death, of reincarnation and karma, and the purpose of life on earth. Followers of White Eagle and the other well-known spirit guides, together with the teachers in the realms of new thought and occultism, all worked hard according to their particular beliefs, but the work was never easy. Before the Second World War there was nothing like the response to spiritual truth, or to new ideas such as the practice of good positive thought and the value of the vegetarian diet, that is so evident at the present time. Vegetarians, Christian Scientists, Spiritualists, followers of any new thought organisation were considered odd or eccentric. Nowadays the boot is entirely on the other foot; experienced workers in the spiritual field find it necessary to restrain enthusiasts from getting into inevitable difficulties by dabbling in occult matters (which can be as dangerous as unguarded electrical appliances are to inquisitive babies).

Apart from the general progress of modern

17

thought one of the factors which has perhaps speeded up men's acceptance of a spiritual reality beyond the confines of the human mind has been the use and abuse of drugs. The use of drugs to bring about altered states of consciousness has long been understood by sages of the ancient civilisations both of the East and West, as well as by the witch doctors of the so-called savage races. It is nothing new. What was new to the Western world was the sudden and widespread experimentation with these drugs, and it brought intense and heart-rending problems to many young people and their parents. Although the results have been tragic for so many individuals, the overall and more lasting effect seems to have been an almost forced opening or widening of the general human consciousness.

While we live a normal life in the physical body we have no idea how limited is the range of the five senses. This is scientifically demonstrated by the colours and the octaves of sound that are quite outside normal perception.

Yet the limits of the human sense organs are a protection to the soul gaining experience in matter. The body is the temple of the spirit and the limitations of the physical senses are like doors of protection, wisely barred until the soul is trained and ready to cope with the

18

wider cosmic picture. The use of certain drugs forces open these protective doors and one or all of the senses becomes expanded, aware of a much wider range of vibrations than the ordinary physical mind believes possible. It seems possible that the widespread distribution of such drugs may have been within the plan for the breaking-down of all kinds of mental limitations, set thought-patterns and habits, set ways of life.

White Eagle prophesied that as the twentieth century proceeded, many souls destined to be leaders and pioneers of the New Age would come into incarnation. A new generation is being born who, looking to the future, to the far broader mental concepts of the Aquarian Age, cannot bear the restrictions, the limitations, the stupidities of the old order. Also the pioneering spirit of youth has made the new generation a ready prey to drugs. Always in life two forces are at work, the positive and negative, the white and the black. When there is a speeding up of the cosmic energies bringing into being a new age, there is an equal speeding up of the powers of light and the powers of darkness. They are like two wheels of a machine which, working against each other, bring about the evolution of mankind.

Thus so many young people born during the

period soon after the Second World War felt driven by an almost inescapable urge to break the bondage of the physical senses, to break out into new worlds, new states of consciousness. Since drugs were fairly easily available and seemed to be an easy way of reaching this exciting, new experience of being, with all the eagerness of youth, and thrilled at defying convention, they took to the drug scene. So their chakras or psychic centres, the protective doors of the physical temple, were flung wide and their unprotected souls bombarded by diverse psychic forces. The exhilaration of this experience filled them with the need to express in sound, beat and colour the enormity, the glory, the excitement, the thrill.

No physical body and nervous system can long stand such pressure, and complete reaction sets in leaving the body listless and quite unable to cope with practical everyday life.

Because this breaking of sense-barriers is a soul-experience quite impossible to describe to someone who has never been through it, it brought about the natural beginnings of another important aspect of the Aquarian Age, the feeling for working and living in groups. The drug takers almost automatically found themselves drawn into groups, apparent dropouts from society who through their forced expansion of consciousness felt deeply that ordinary materialistic values are a great illusion; and that true brotherhood, widespread brotherhood, was the new order. But many other young people, and some older people too, are being drawn together in communities, trying to discover together the secret of communal living. In actual fact this is nothing like as easy as it seems. As one gets down to practical everyday living one comes up against the same old difficulties, the same personality problems, that are part of all human experience, part of the eternal discipline of the shining spirit striving to purify, manipulate and beautify matter.

Throughout the ages, spiritual teachers and gurus of every race warn their pupils against the use of drugs, alcohol or stimulants which can affect or derange the nervous system and cause the conscious mind to lose control. The casualties of the drug scene are only too well-known to doctors and social workers in the Western world. Among those who have been sufficiently strong in spirit to survive the forced expansion of their consciousness are quite a number who, having caught a glimpse of the tremendous scene beyond and within the physical life, have felt impelled to set their feet on a path of spiritual training and unfoldment, a path of self-discipline and aspiration—in fact the same road towards the golden world of God that all the saints have trod before them.

What is the essential difference between the 'high' of drug experience, and the state of samadhi, that spiritual ecstasy achieved by the saints? There is no doubt that a certain type of mystic experience, even some kind of elevating inner vision can temporarily be obtained by drug taking, but the essential difference between this and the heavenly consciousness that can be reached in meditation is that the latter is entirely under the control of the operator. Success comes as a result of spiritual and physical discipline, through efforts to purify the life and the thought and through steadfast aspiration over a long period. In fact it has to be earned; but once the meditator has learned how to raise his consciousness to a certain level he can always repeat the experience. He knows the rules; he knows the way, and can rise into the higher worlds or come down at will.

Of course on some days the ascent will be easier than others. *The wind bloweth where it listeth, and thou hearest the sound thereof, but canst not tell whence it cometh, and whither it goeth.* Sometimes, there seems to come a special dispensation from above, like a heavenly baptism; but always the meditator remains in control. He

22

can return at will to the physical life, ensure that his psychic centres are properly sealed, and take up his worldly responsibilities with renewed zest and courage, and with deeper understanding. The spiritual contact made during meditation helps him to live a better life, to be of greater service to his companions and to appreciate more fully all God's gifts. J. Stanley White says in his book *Liberation of the Soul*, 'A man steeped in inner-revelation generates peace and tranquillity all about him. He is a source of strength and happiness to others and becomes, as Christ put it, a light shining before men.'

On the other hand the induced expansion of consciousness in the psychedelic 'trip' is entirely outside the control of the individual. Once the drug is taken he cannot come off 'high' until the effects on his nervous system and the etheric body have worn off. The resulting psychic strain leaves him limp and uninterested in the physical life, and unwilling and unable to cope with his responsibilities. He can become a liability to family and friends.

In meditation, we learn to still the physical senses, the emotions and the outer mind in order to bring into action that truer consciousness which White Eagle calls 'the mind in the heart'. Psychedelics, the so-called mind-manifesting drugs, work in just the opposite way, by intensifying the physical senses and expanding the mind, making it superactive and uncontrolled, rather than quiescent and at peace. They contravene the ancient rules of spiritual unfoldment and are bound to involve their takers in troubles of many kinds, not the least of which is having to cope, in a weakened physical state, with an extraordinarily enhanced sensitivity.

We find on studying the lives and the writings of the great mystics of any age or race that they all give us, in essence, the same message. There may be minor differences in their experiences and modes of expression, but by and large they all describe the same stages of spiritual unfoldment. The path to God-consciousness is well marked with the same signposts, the same experiences. Indeed it is often most comforting to those who are struggling along the road to discover that they are part of a goodly company, who share the same struggles, tests and heartaches, the same moments of illumination and heavenly joy.

On the other hand, from descriptions of drug experiences it seems that no two are alike, nor can a specific experience be repeated at will. Many people have reported some kind of mystical vision, but dose after dose of the drug will not produce a repeat performance, which is unsatisfying and tantalising—so different from that sense of deep peace and inner joy which results from the regular discipline of meditation.

Naturally the rapid growth in scientific knowledge and education generally has caused the old religious dogmas to be subjected to severe scrutiny. The ones which prove inadequate to meet modern needs are ruthlessly discarded. These far-reaching changes and apparent moral decadence need cause no dismay to those who have knowledge of the Ancient Wisdom. The New Age will bring to humanity a fresh illumination and a restatement of the ageless truth, to suit current needs. Jesus said, *no man putteth new wine into old bottles*. The new ideals of the Aquarian Age need new religious concepts and forms.

Aquarius is the sign of friendship, brotherhood and group projects, as well as of scientific development and conquest of space. The old superstitions and conventions which have been the cause of so much cruelty and suffering are rapidly passing, and the religion of the New Age will inevitably be one of true brotherhood, friendship and co-operation.

If man will follow the spiritual guidance which is even now coming to him from many sources, if he will learn to live in accordance with cosmic law, he will go steadily forward into a new era of happiness and achievement.

As surely as the seasons of the small solar year follow the movement of the sun, so do the seasons of man's evolution follow the progress of the sun's vernal point through the constellations. The long dark 'winter of our discontent' is even now giving place to the increasing light and joy of a spring which in turn will pass into the full summer of the Great Year; a new golden age of brotherhood, peace and perfect health.

2. The Cosmic Christ

The history of Christianity at the beginning of the Piscean Age bears witness not only to the emotional and mystical aspect of the Piscean influence, but also to the confusion and muddle which is usually associated with this sign. As the Christian teaching spread through Europe and Asia Minor, it became, for instance, curiously mixed with the local cults of Mithraism, based on sun-worship, and took over many of its rites and festivals. In no respect was the confusion greater than in what men believed about who Jesus was, how far he was man and how far he was God.

Eventually so many diverse doctrines were held by different groups scattered all over the Roman Empire, that the leaders of the Church called a series of councils in order to standardise Christian belief. Thus, at the Council of Nicaea in AD 325, the doctrine of the divinity of Jesus was established by majority vote. This decision not only divorced Christianity from the teaching of the Ancient Wisdom concerning the Cosmic Christ, but led to further dis-

27

tortion and misunderstanding of much of the teaching of Jesus and the apostles concerning Christ's redeeming power.

According to the Ancient Wisdom the physical sun is an outward and visible sign of a timeless spirit, glorious beyond human conception, source of all life. As the earth depends for sustenance on the light and warmth of the visible sun, so do men's souls depend for their life, evolution and happiness on the invisible sun, which St John described as *the true Light, which lighteth every man that cometh into the world.*

Christ, third principle of Godhead, is the Light that is the sun, visible in this respect, but infinitely more radiant and beautiful than the physical sun. It is impossible to convey in language, or even to conceive or imagine, an idea of his glory and magnificence. We cannot picture him solely in the semblance of a man, for this is to give limitation to his being; and Christ, though he is indeed the ideal form of mankind, is to the ordinary human being as the mountain is to the speck of sand on the seashore. This Light, whose aura encloses the earth and penetrates far beyond it, the vibration of whose being is the life of all existence on suns and planets, surpasses our comprehension. Yet a spark of it, an incipient flame, is within every man, woman and child; and because of this each man, made in God's image, can become godlike.

This Light, the Christ in men's hearts, takes many ages to stir and quicken, as though it were a seed in the dark earth. Nevertheless in each man, in the course of innumerable lives on earth, it grows in radiance until it begins to dominate the thick darkness of flesh and blood, the darkness that 'comprehended it not'. The Ancient Wisdom teaches that man is born on earth in a coat of flesh not once but many times, until the spirit that is buried in darkness awakens and grows strong enough to transmute the physical particles into light itself.

When this stage is reached, the soul is freed from the necessity to reincarnate and becomes a Master or Christed One. From time to time such great souls voluntarily reincarnate in order to demonstrate to struggling humanity the glory and the simplicity of the Christ Light.

The power of the flame grows by slow degrees; but at a certain stage in the evolutionary cycle it begins to illumine the outer consciousness. The man or woman begins to feel an inner urge to seek and find truth, and when this happens he is led, often in quite an extraordinary way, to people who will help or books which will enlighten him. Then experiences come which stimulate the inner light and cause it to develop more rapidly. The individual enters upon the path of aspiration and self-discipline. Saints and seers of every age and religion have followed this path of initiation. Jesus of Nazareth was an initiate, perhaps one above all others.

According to the Ancient Wisdom, however, the Cosmic Christ cannot be identified with any one personality, although throughout the ancient world, among many races besides the Jews, there were prophecies concerning the time when the Light would shine in darkness and the Word would be made flesh and dwell among men. As we have seen, Jesus was born practically at the mid-point of the Great Year. This was a most powerful time, astrologically, when the vernal point was near the cusp of the constellation Aries, in which the sun is exalted. The time had come in the evolutionary cycle for humanity as a whole to receive the baptism of the Cosmic Christ, which would quicken the Light in all men. Hitherto the emphasis in religion had been on the power-aspect of the deity. During the 'childhood' of humanity racial instincts were very strong and man's conception of God was limited to the image of a strong man of his own people. Yet the inspired prophets, who looked beyond such limitations, foresaw the coming of one who would awaken men more fully to their own real needs and the needs of others, and inspire the selfless devotion that alone could bring into actuality the ideal of universal brotherhood.

This was the special mission for which Jesus had been prepared through many incarnations; to be an instrument through which the Cosmic Christ could find human expression and work among us, not only during his public mission of three years, but as an example and a presence throughout the Age which followed. For with the coming of the special personification of the Christ Light through Jesus of Nazareth there also came a great solar baptism of humanity itself, and from that time dates man's departure from the old racial spirit towards the new spirit of love and peace and brotherhood.

It is interesting that in the New Testament, baptism both by water and the spirit is brought into such prominence, in view of the influence of the watery sign of Pisces. One of the characteristics of this sign is psychic receptivity, and the soul of humanity was at this time especially prepared and ready to receive the baptism of the Cosmic Christ, 'earthed', as it were, through the personality of Jesus.

The development of early Christianity was marked by other unmistakable signs of the Piscean Age. The symbol of the fishes is dual, and duality soon manifested in the division of the early Christians into two main sections, not only the purely physical division of the Eastern and the Roman Churches, but a subtler division of the exoteric, or outer, and the esoteric, or inner, interpretation of the Christian teaching. The Church, following St Peter, taught the outer symbolism of the new religion. Its adherents gradually formed a well-organised priesthood promulgating a clear-cut Christian faith, which has held sway over Western civilisation. In this exoteric form of religion the concept of the divinity of Jesus was substituted for the teaching of the Ancient Wisdom concerning the Cosmic Christ.

The second group of early Christians consisted of small circles or brotherhoods scattered in many parts of the world who worked in secret to keep the truths of the Ancient Wisdom alive. The founder and leader of these groups was St John, the mystic, who in his gospel, epistles and book of Revelation presents an aspect of the teachings of Jesus which differs considerably from that of the other evangelists. When his gospel is read in the light of the Ancient Wisdom concerning the Cosmic Christ, much that was hitherto confusing becomes clear. The book of Revelation deals symbolically with the evolution of the spirit of humanity in all its phases, through the great Ages of the constellation zodiac. These mystical teachings were transmitted to an inner brotherhood of St John.

Despite the centuries of cruelty and confusion these inner brotherhoods have persisted, handing down the secret teachings of mystical Christianity to those ready to accept them, and guarding their knowledge even in the face of death and persecution. These brothers of the mystical Christianity strove to demonstrate in their lives the precepts of Jesus. Wherever they went they were loved and revered for their simplicity, kindness and true saintliness. One group, known as the Albigenses, was persecuted to the point of extinction by Church and State. Yet the line of light has been held through the centuries and now, at the beginning of the new Age of Aquarius, the White Brethren both visible and invisible are becoming increasingly active. All over the world they work, still in small groups, to give those who are spiritually hungry the mystical Christian teachings which will satisfy their deepest needs and supply the practical answer to their most tormenting problems.

In the final chapter of St John's gospel, after the occurrence of the miraculous draught of fishes, St Peter asked Jesus what was to be the future work of St John, the beloved. He received the answer, *If I will that he tarry till I come, what is that to thee? follow thou me.* Thus did Jesus outline the work of these two disciples. St Peter was to 'feed my sheep', he was to 'shepherd' the people, to give them a presentation of Christianity which would supply their needs while they were developing a certain mystical understanding and faith through their belief in Jesus as a personal redeemer. The idea of the Christ as a cosmic or universal Being who became 'earthed' through Jesus was quite beyond the comprehension of the masses. They needed the 'shepherding' or organisation of the Church of St Peter. But the few who could comprehend the mystical teaching of the Cosmic Christ remained in small, secret communities under the guidance of St John until, in the symbolism of the gospel, the man carrying the pitcher of water—Aquarius—would lead them to the upper room where they would commune with Christ.

As the influence of the Aquarian Age grows stronger, the mystical Christianity of St John will gradually replace the outworn orthodoxy of the church of Peter. It will lead humanity to 'an upper room'—a higher state of consciousness or comprehension—where true communion with the Cosmic Christ will come to all who earnestly seek. It will lead the seeker to the Holy Grail which brings healing for all sorrow and pain. As understanding of this true communion becomes universal, the light of the Cosmic Christ shining through men's hearts and lives will glorify the earth itself. This is the promised second coming of Christ, foreshadowed in the gospels.

3. The Cosmic Laws governing Human Life

In AD 553 the Church Council of Constantinople decreed that anyone who supported the 'mythical' doctrine of the pre-existence of the soul and believed in the soul's return to earth after death should henceforth be anathema. Thus again by majority vote the church leaders suppressed a truth of the Ancient Wisdom implicit in the teachings of Jesus and taught in the mystery schools throughout the ancient world. Reincarnation is the accepted belief of millions in the East today.

As we have seen, the Church had its own mission to fulfil in the evolution of humanity. Nevertheless, a church that claims to be the sole receiver and dispenser of truth, with power to afford salvation by means of the sacraments or to refuse them and condemn men to eternal and unmitigable pain, can exercise a terrible hold over men's imagination. Such doctrine must tend to take away any sense of personal responsibility and lead to the conclusion that a man can do what he will and get away with it, so long as he has means to pay the price exacted by the priesthood.

With the growth of scientific knowledge in the Western world and the awakening of a social conscience in men generally, it is small wonder that many people can no longer accept such ideas, and that the whole authority of the Church is questioned. Most people long for some understanding of the meaning of life and death, but they no longer have faith in the ability of the Church to answer their problems.

White Eagle teaches that life on earth is governed by five immutable laws. It is impossible to give here a full account of these laws and their outworking, but the following indications may be helpful.

1. *Reincarnation, the Law of Rebirth*

In short, life in the physical body is like a term at school. We come back to the earth with certain lessons to learn, certain gifts to develop, and at the end of term we go home again, or withdraw to an inner or more subtle state of being in what may be called a 'land of light', for a period of rest and refreshment. During this time, the soul can review what was gained or lost in the life now finished. When it has had a period of rest and refreshment and feels the urge to gain more wisdom, it is shown the next set of lessons to be learnt, and drawn into incarnation at the appropriate time and place. This process of labour and refreshment continues until the whole earth-curriculum is completed.

2. *Karma, the Law of Cause and Effect*

This is the law that we receive back the exact results of our actions. St Paul said, *Be not deceived; God is not mocked: for whatsoever a man soweth, that shall he also reap.*

Under precise, inexorable law, and by God's supreme justice, we are reborn in an environment where we meet again those whom we have wronged or been wronged by, and those whom we have helped or been helped by, in the past. We incarnate with those we have injured until all wrongs have been put right and all hurts forgiven; until all hate or jealousy has been transmuted to love. We reincarnate also with those whom we have loved and been loved by; and this brings joy into our lives. By God's mercy we may, if we will to do so, turn all that we suffer into strength, and so make creative use of our own 'bad karma' at a higher level of experience. Everyone has frustrations and sorrows, which are due to past mistakes and beyond their power to alter; but

38

everyone has power in the present to shape their future limitations or opportunities by their thoughts and actions now.

3. *The Law of Opportunity*

This law is closely linked with the laws of reincarnation and karma. It ensures that the reincarnating soul is drawn to the circumstances which will bring opportunities to pay off old debts and acquire the knowledge and experience that is sought. This is freewill operating under constraints which the soul chooses and accepts; for although our present life grows out of the past and is limited by past mistakes we have in us the power to shape the future out of the very difficulties that confront us. The flame of Christ in the heart of every human being has Christ's creative powers. If we can learn to bring it into operation we shall find that it has a magical effect both on ourselves and our surroundings. We can learn so to control and direct our thoughts and feelings that they create instead of destroy and so that we comfort and heal rather than thoughtlessly condemn those about us. Indeed, in some incarnations where heavy debts are being paid off, this may be the only plane on which whatever power of freewill we have can work.

It may encourage those who suffer crippling

39

and apparently incurable disease, sorrow or frustration to know that there is a positive, hopeful aspect of their situation. For they can either accept the self-imposed limitations with patience and fortitude and, rising above self-pity, strive to use thought and creative imagination in such a way as to bring joy and inspiration to others; or they can give up the struggle and sink ever deeper into self-pity and resentment, making life miserable for everyone else in their environment. If the former course is chosen, not only is the debt more rapidly paid, but the soul gains strength and vision. This is fruitful use of karmic opportunity, opening as it does the prospect of responsible work in a healthy body in a fresh incarnation.

This Law of Opportunity works also in our natural inclination to develop skill in the arts and sciences. We feel an instinctive interest in subjects we have studied and enjoyed in the past, and according to the measure we have worked and persevered to acquire techniques, we return with an apparently 'natural gift', which we can improve by further application. Conversely, wasted or misused opportunities are withdrawn, as in the parable of the talents.

Divine law is just, perfect and true in every detail.

4. *The Law of Balance and Equilibrium*

The manifestation of this law is apparent throughout nature in such phenomena as day and night, heat and cold, expansion and contraction, positive and negative currents, the chemical balance between acid and alkali, the swing of the pendulum even. It is a fundamental law regarding the human mind and body which acts as a safeguard, ensuring that extremism can only be carried so far before reaction sets in and pulls us back to normal. This law is especially interesting in connection with the development of the personality in successive incarnations, as it causes the soul to swing between poles, for instance between introvert and extrovert activity, until a perfectly balanced expression is reached. It may cause a soul which has been fanatical in one incarnation to be just as fanatical in the opposite direction in another, in order to adjust the soul's equilibrium. Joy and sorrow in human experience tend to follow this law, which may also be described as a law of compensation. True philosophers are well aware that sorrow always carves deeper channels for joy.

5. *The Law of Correspondences*

This law implies a peculiarly close relationship between man the microcosm, and God the macrocosm. We can only begin to understand it when we realise that all outer and visible manifestation is the result of an inner and invisible will or creative urge; in other words, of thought. The whole manifested universe is the result of God's thought, and man, made in God's image, possesses in embryo God's creative powers. He is himself a god in the making.

The Law of Correspondences is also a law of externalisation, whereby the state of our inner consciousness gradually and inevitably externalises itself in the physical body. When a child is born, deep in the recesses of its inner self there is a programme showing how the life should unfold. This plan is stamped also on various parts of the body such as the palms of the hands and the bumps on the head. It is implicit in the handwriting, in how the person walks and in every form of expression, so that a trained seer, one who understands how to interpret the signs, can judge fairly accurately the soul's character and destiny during the present life. Observant doctors can often diagnose, according to physical type and build, the diseases to which patients may be liable.

Similarly, there is a mysterious linking of man's character and circumstances with the position in the heavens of the sun, moon and planets at the moment of birth. The sacred science of astrology formed a part of the Ancient Wisdom, and is well worth the serious attention of the modern student.

Ancient philosophers expressed the Law of Correspondences in the words, 'As above, so below; as in heaven, so on earth', and herein lies a valuable key to the study of spiritual science. When the full implications of this law are realised one cannot but be overcome with wonder at the majesty of the divine wisdom and love behind every detail of human life.

4. The Five Laws in Daily Life

Loving God

An understanding of the five Laws just enumerated is of the greatest value in daily life. By adjusting his thoughts and actions in order to live harmoniously with these laws, the individual finds that increased harmony and beauty begin to manifest in his outer circumstances. All crooked places are gradually made straight.

Moses, in the Old Testament story, gave ten commandments, all designed to help men to live harmoniously within the framework of spiritual law. Jesus condensed these into two precepts which are as true and powerful now as on the day they were uttered. The first of these was, *Thou shalt love the Lord thy God with all thy heart, and with all thy soul, and with all thy mind.* He added, *This is the first and great commandment.*

The observance of this fundamental principle brings peace and happiness and gives meaning to existence. Loving God is something much more joyous and vital than orthodox religious worship. Quite simply it means loving and reverencing life itself. St John said, '*No man hath seen God at any time*', yet God, or the manifestation of God in Christ the Son, is the divine invisible fire or light within every living creature. When we begin to open our eyes to the beauty and wonder in nature, when we begin to appreciate the joy of human companionship, or the pleasure of creating some beautiful or useful object, we are unconsciously loving God, and putting ourselves in harmony with this precept. Any activity that brings with it a sense of delight, a sense of self-respect, is awakening in us a love of God.

As soon as we love life itself and find happiness in all the gifts it brings, we love God. Love means serving. A man cannot truly love without desiring to serve the object of his love. The more we love life, the more we feel the desire to serve it by creating beauty in our surroundings. This God-given urge can be nurtured daily until the desire to serve life in all its forms becomes a force which motivates every action.

Every man, woman and child has a deeply felt need to create something which will add to the composite beauty of life. Any work performed wholeheartedly and well brings joy and satisfaction quite apart from the material reward. It brings an inner glow of happiness which releases fresh sources of strength for greater effort and achievement. It is well known that muscles in the body which are constantly used grow strong and powerful, while those which do no work become flabby and in time atrophy.

Whatsoever thy hand findeth to do, do it with thy might is another biblical precept which shows how to express the love of God, or good in life. No matter what form service takes, so long as it is given wholeheartedly, without thought of reward, it is an expression of goodwill, or God-will, and releases inner springs of joy and energy. Tending a garden, beautifying a home, baking a cake, making machinery run smoothly and efficiently, caring for the sick and needy are all creative activities expressing man's love of God; indeed any work which makes life easier and more harmonious for others is such an expression.

To obey this first and greatest command-ment is to put ourselves in harmony with spir-itual law, and so to create good karma, which surely brings ever-widening opportunities, ever-increasing power to achieve. In the par-able of the talents the two servants who worked to increase their talents did so not for personal gain, but to serve their master; whereas the one who buried his talent feared and resented his master and refused to exert himself on his behalf, so he lost even what he had.

Sometimes workers resent the fact that their labour puts money into the pocket of their employer; they grumble because they do not get what they consider to be a fair share of the profits. Knowledge of the laws of reincarnation, karma, and opportunity will help them to realise that the relationship of employer to worker is the outworking in this incarnation of some similar relationship, possibly with the positions reversed, in the past. Ultimately man's responsibility for service is not to any other man, but to God, to the light in his own heart which is one with the spiritual Sun. He must give his very best to his work if he would increase and strengthen that light. Another man's injustice is not his business, but giving his own best efforts in service is. This wholehearted self-giving to life brings abundant reward, for God has his own way of giving just payment to those who serve for sheer love of life. Jesus expressed this truth in the words, *He that findeth his life shall lose it: and he that loseth his life for my sake shall find it.*

Love for God may or may not find expression in formal worship in church or chapel.

Such formal worship is not necessary; but as our realisation of the perfect outworking of spiritual law deepens and grows, we can find increased inspiration and strength by joining with others in recognising and worshipping the source of all life.

All service undertaken wholeheartedly presents challenges; as soon as one problem is solved another presents itself. In facing these problems we gradually discover how to derive strength and wisdom by turning inwards to worship our creator. Such worship should never become a stale duty, but should be a spontaneous looking to the spiritual Sun for sustenance. In worship we open our souls to God or Christ as flowers do to the sunlight, and we receive all that we need in mind or soul or body.

Modern man has been taught to regard sun-worship as a pagan belief; but when we recall what sunlight means to the life of the earth, when we realise that God, the Universal Spirit, is the life-giving force behind the sun, we begin to understand what sun-worship really means. The spirit of God is like the warmth of the sun, life-giving, healing, drawing forth beauty from the earth. In the measure that the sun reigns in our heart, we radiate warmth and goodwill.

Recognising the source of all joy, our hearts

overflow in thankfulness, in worship of the Great Spirit; we cannot but love God as Father and Mother with all our heart, all our mind and all our strength.

Human Relationships

The second commandment that Jesus gave was, *Thou shalt love thy neighbour as thyself.*

In this principle lies the key to many of the problems of karma, which demand patience, self-discipline, humour and imagination, not only in life's big issues, but in the small details of human relationships at home and at work. Many people make the mistake of thinking that the Law of Karma affects only the dramatic issues; they do not realise that every thought, word and action in daily life creates or destroys their future health and happiness. For instance, habitual criticism or condemnation gradually builds up, later to rebound on the critic, who in the present life or a future one may suffer agonies of self-doubt, even to the point of mental breakdown, while every genuine effort to bring kindly encouragement, happiness and cheer to others helps to build for the future a strong, resilient yet sensitive nervous system with potential for happy creativity.

The working of the Law of Karma is exact, perfect and true. Stated at its crudest, it means

49

that we must all experience within our own being the same suffering or joy that we have brought to others, whether on the physical, mental or emotional plane. But it is so much more than this: it is the educative process by which man gradually learns to use his freewill and innate creative power for Godlike purposes. To take a few of the simpler patterns in the complexity of human relationships, a man who has caused physical suffering to another or ridiculed him, may be born with a defect similar to that which he caused or ridiculed; he will feel in his own body and mind what he inflicted. Only by learning what it feels like to be hurt and rejected can we begin to imagine how our actions will affect those about us. On the positive side, spending ourselves in loving service, making life for those in our environment as happy and rewarding as possible, inevitably builds into our own future health and opportunity.

Again, indifference to the pain and suffering of others, turning a blind eye or a deaf ear to a cry for help, can eventually manifest in deafness or eye trouble. This is by no means to say that all blindness or deafness springs from such a cause, but those who suffer such hardship may well regard it as an opportunity to become more alert, through their remaining senses, to the needs of others. Also, the more deaf and blind they are to worldly concerns, the more alert and sensitive they may become to spiritual realities.

Close human relationships, whether happy or wretched, are never accidental, but always the outworking of karmic law. We reincarnate in groups with those we have loved and those we have hated, rather as pupils return with the rest of their school class after the holidays, except that the return occurs not on one day, but within a span of years which allows those who have incurred debts in a certain human relationship to restore the balance within a similar relationship, or with the positions reversed. For instance, parents who have neglected, ill-used or bullied their children may find themselves suffering similar treatment during a subsequent childhood.

An over-indulgent parent can cause unhappiness not only to the child, but to that child's future colleagues, friends, marriage partner and children. It is pleasant to gratify the wishes of a beloved child, but it takes more strength of character to train the child, through wise self-discipline, to live fully and happily. Many a soul who now suffers through a selfish, irresponsible partner may well in a past life have been one of that person's parents, and through

51

over-indulgence have encouraged the very traits which now bring pain. When life brings us the responsibility of guiding and training another soul, it must be recognised as a serious obligation.

Any desertion of helpless dependants incurs a karmic debt which may be worked off when the soul suffers the deep human longing to be necessary to someone, and yet is deprived of all close family ties. Feeling this need the soul is often given the opportunity to make good the balance by devoting the life to serving others in some way, possibly by nursing the sick, by teaching children, by faithfully ministering to the public in some basic need. Always, thoughtlessness and neglect must be made good and the balance restored.

These facts need not depress those who are now suffering sadness, loneliness or physical disability, for God is merciful and loving as well as just. Together with the Law of Karma there is another just as vital: the Law of Opportunity. This means that every trying, agonising circumstance is an opportunity for building and creating positive good for the future.

To avail ourselves of the opportunity, we must fight to overcome self-pity and resentment against people and circumstances. We must meet each day's trials with all we can muster of fortitude and laughter. Jesus showed the only true and practical way to rise above resentment and to make full use of opportunity when he said *Bless them that curse you, do good to them that hate you, and pray for them which despitefully use you, and persecute you.*

In human relations two important lessons have to be learnt: the wise use of power, and the wise direction of emotion. It takes the experience of many, many incarnations for a soul to gain the wisdom needed to control and balance these two forces so that they are used creatively and not for self-gratification. In every human relationship there is ideally a certain balance of power, subtly combined with emotion. In a truly harmonious life this balance is recognised and carefully maintained.

Certain relationships, such as that of parent and child, teacher and pupil, employer and employee, necessitate an uneven balance of power between the individuals concerned. In all such cases, the one invested with power must learn to wield it with wisdom, kindness and a keen sense of responsibility, while the one who is subservient must learn to be obedient, conscientious and loyal, giving due respect and gratitude for the security and training given.

So much suffering can be caused through

thoughtlessness and lack of imagination. Even kindly people are sometimes hopelessly blind to the fact that they are causing suffering to those in their power through carelessness or laziness. Unfortunately, the possession of power is like strong drink and, upsetting the balance, tempts a soul to be ruthless and sometimes cruel. Yet any suffering caused to others will rebound either in this life or a future one. The law is exact and inescapable.

The same law of course applies positively. When power is used kindly and wisely, the soul will be reborn with those gifts, nurtured by wise use, even more fully developed. Opportunities may appear to come to such souls automatically, and whatever they do seems favoured with 'good luck'. Yet there is no such thing as good luck, only exact recompense. Even then, since life is eternally progressive, apparent 'good luck' is a further test of the soul's ability to use its gifts wisely, perhaps on a different plane of expression.

Unbridled emotion can have as devastating an effect on human happiness as the overbalance of power. Excess of feeling which is mistakenly called love, often means possessiveness or selfish desire and can easily turn to hate. Uncontrolled emotion is in fact another form of self-indulgence, and through it others suffer.

In the man–woman relationship, each possesses power in a different way. Through the ages women have suffered much through men's physical superiority and domination, but they in their turn can cause acute misery to men through the misuse of their magnetic and emotional power. Again, the true balance has eventually to be found, whereby in the New Age men and women will work in partnership and mutual respect each supplying some quality needed by the other.

Friendship in the ideal sense is a result of mutual attraction, mutual interests, and an equal balance of power which gives mutual independence. This relationship should bring joy to both, yet leave both completely free. As soon as one tries to bind or possess the other emotionally, the relationship ceases to be friendship and may indicate some imbalance from the past which needs to be brought into true focus. Unhappiness in any human relationship is the result of such an imbalance of power and emotion between the two souls in the past. But when the one who has wielded power unwisely is placed in a position of difficult subservience in the present incarnation, the experience thus gained gradually brings a truer understanding of the relationship.

In love or friendship, to arouse and then

treat lightly the feelings of another, must always create unhappy karma. Sexual behaviour and morality differ with geographical location, but the spiritual law which governs human relationships is exact, eternal and unalterable. It is found stated in various ways in all the great religions: behave to all others as you, in a similar situation, would like them to behave towards you. Imagination, above all, is the quality needed in relationships.

There is yet another balance, however, which we have to preserve. Sometimes, in our efforts to be kind and to serve others, we are over-conscientious, trying to give more than physical strength permits. Proper balance of work, rest and recreation is essential both for physical and mental health. If this balance is not kept, our powers either for service or enjoyment will be gradually impaired. For the commandment says, *Thou shalt love thy neighbour as thyself*—no more, no less. The laws of karma are subtle but exact and are based on the innermost motive for thought and action, whether it is selfish and arrogant or kind and caring.

These truths are simple, but by no means easy to apply in daily life. There are five rules which, if observed, will help to create or restore the harmonious balance in human relationships.

1. *Remember always the dignity of the spirit*

As we have already seen, within every soul burns a flame of God, part of the being of the Cosmic Christ. Therefore in all our dealings, whether they be with children or adults, men with power or men who depend on us, men of our own country or another, we must look for and respect that inmost flame of the spirit, no matter how much the outer appearance may seem to belie its existence. Knowledge of the laws of reincarnation and karma gives fresh significance to the old-fashioned rules of courtesy and chivalry which make for happy human relationships. Even from the most selfish angle they are worthwhile. Springing as they do from consideration and thoughtfulness, these rules ensure that those who observe them will themselves receive consideration when they most need it. True courtesy beautifies all human relationships.

2. *Accept the responsibilities of each different human relationship that your karma brings*

Inevitably we find ourselves at various times responsible for the happiness and well-being of many different people. Each relationship carries its own privileges and duties; and they must be accepted even if the other person seems unresponsive or ungrateful.

When any human relationship proves disappointing, it is worth remembering that although we may now be reaping what we sowed, we can restore the balance and create joy for the future by faithfully and cheerfully fulfilling our obligations. By striving to bring happiness to those concerned, we can rebuild what we have thoughtlessly broken down in the past.

3. *Quickly forgive the sins and omissions of others and cultivate a tender compassion for all human faults*

All of us, while chained to the wheel of rebirth, badly need each other's compassion. True forgiveness releases the soul from the chain of karmic reaction. When a wrong has been committed against another, a pendulum is set in motion, bringing opportunity for revenge first to one and then to the other protagonist. This continues sometimes with increasing ferocity, until at last one of the parties freely forgives and returns kindness for harshness, compassion for cruelty.

In practice it is often easier to forgive big dramatic wrongs than the small irritations of daily existence, which constitute our real karma.

It's the little things of life that put us on a rack.
You can sit upon a mountain, but not upon a tack.

These little rubs can be much eased by a tender understanding of human frailty. So often people may seem bad-tempered and difficult when really they are strained and unhappy or in a low state of health. None can know the burden of another's karma. Even when people are selfish, greedy and ill-natured they merit compassion, since they are busily creating future misery for themselves.

When Jesus said on the cross, *Father, forgive them; for they know not what they do*, he could see clearly the long train of karma which his tormentors, in their ignorance, were creating for themselves, and his compassion enfolded them. The memory of this would in fact work so deeply in their souls that when in the future these men found themselves in a similar position, at the mercy of ignorance and injustice, the memory could awaken this same impulse to forgive, which would in turn bless and release both persecutor and sufferer.

4. *Guard your speech*

More real unhappiness and more difficult karma is created by idle tongues than by almost any other factor in human relationships. It is so fatally easy to speak the clever, mocking words, with a sting in them, to voice negative, destructive criticism; or to pass on gossip just slightly twisted and dramatised. But if we could see the karmic result of these destructive words we would wish we had been struck dumb before we uttered them. Karmically, we are held responsible for the full effect of our words upon others, and all damage done has to be healed before we are free to progress. Moreover, the spoken or written word can have immense power over the minds of others. Writers take full karmic responsibility for the words they speak, the images they project, the characters they let loose.

In *The Return of Arthur Conan Doyle*, Sir Arthur says, 'Some day every man will attain either the joy or the terror of seeing the effect of his creations, beautiful or the reverse; no matter whether they are merely fictitious characters or actual conditions of life resulting from actions of his which have considerably influenced the lives of others.'

5. *Cultivate a sense of humour and gaiety*

It is all too easy in human relationships to make mountains out of molehills and to take small frets too seriously. Our daily struggles and irritations are highly transient when viewed in the light of eternity. In India it is believed that the soul reincarnates 840,000 times. This may or may not be true, but certainly it takes many, many life-experiences before the Christ spirit within achieves mastery over the outer, worldly man, and over the physical body and its environment.

Laughter and a sense of fun ease the journey for ourselves and our companions. Nature is full of laughter; sunlight on the water, the frolics of the wind, the exuberance of young creatures even though sometimes these capers may be in the face of danger: all these illustrate the gaiety and courage of natural life.

There is nearly always a funny side to the karmic situations in which we find ourselves. Training ourselves to see this will lighten the load, and help us to keep a sense of proportion.

Needless to say, any kind of mockery or ridicule of others is in quite a different category and has nothing to do with that sense of merriment which is part of the courage of a soul facing adversity.

5. Death and the Hereafter

Acceptance of the truth of reincarnation brings a very different view of the death of the physical body. Instead of being the gate of no return, death can be seen as an incident, a recurring event in a long life-cycle.

Some most interesting experiments with hypnosis have been conducted in this century, whereby psychologists have tried to probe the subconscious mind of an individual by directing it backwards into its own past, even to events before birth. The results leave little doubt that beneath the normal daily consciousness lie memories which reach far back into former lives and deaths.

In the myths of Greece and Rome, the soul was supposed to journey across the River Styx to the Underworld. The soul was guided on its way by Mercury, who in astrological symbolism represents the mind or consciousness; and before souls could return from the Underworld to the earth, they had to drink of the waters of Lethe, or forgetfulness.

62

If, as the experiments suggest, many memories of past lives are shut off from the conscious mind, the picture of the soul drinking the 'waters of forgetfulness' before coming back into incarnation presents a clear idea of what must in fact take place. The distress sometimes suffered by the subjects of these hypnotic experiments as they delved into the immediate past shows how merciful is the provision that we cannot remember former lives. This does not mean that we cannot benefit by lessons learned through them. These remain with us as apparently instinctive reactions to certain situations; instinctive likes, dislikes and aptitudes.*

An impartial study of books such as those recommended here (on pages 132–3) should convince the reader that man's survival after death, and his ability thereafter to communicate with those still 'in a coat of skin', is a proven fact. Yet the best and safest way of

* It must be emphasised that regression under hypnosis is a process that should only be used with wisdom and discrimination by qualified specialists. In certain cases it could have therapeutic effects, but should never be used just to satisfy curiosity. White Eagle teaches that memories of the past awaken naturally at the right time and should not be forced.

communicating with those who have passed onward is yet to be fully understood.

The Aquarian Age was heralded by rapid advances in scientific discovery and invention, and with these, a tendency to intellectual materialism in the Western world. That these barriers of materialism should be broken down was an indispensable preparation for the re-statement of the Ancient Wisdom that is needed in the New Age. Because of this, the movement known as Modern Spiritualism was brought into being under the direction of the White Brotherhood, with whose help the early pioneers of the movement withstood severe opposition and persecution while they pro-duced the proofs of survival which humanity so sorely needed.

The stage of the Spiritualist work which was intended to give the world visible and audible proof of the after-life through physical pheno-mena seems to be passing. There are now many fewer good 'physical' mediums and psy-chic photographers than there were. Some of the well-known spirit guides have now with-drawn from their public work. Many people, while fully convinced of the fact of survival, say, 'What next?'

White Eagle, from the very beginning of his ministry, discouraged any form of 'physical' phenomenon in his Lodge. He teaches that to dabble in such phenomena without knowledge of the laws which govern them is as dangerous as an amateur dabbling with electrical installations. As we have said, these phenomena were produced for a time only, to shake man out of his materialism and awaken him to occult truths. Now the need for this stimulation is passing and those who have been so awakened must be ready for the next and more difficult step, not lightly to be taken, which is to learn to unfold for themselves, and within themselves, an awareness of the inner, or higher, worlds. This can only be done with prayer and self-discipline; but everyone has the power to quicken and enlarge the scope of his consciousness and to hold communion, not only with those who no longer have a physical body, but with guides and teachers who can help them in their work and service on earth.

The astral world in which man awakens after death may be described as an inner or finer world. This world is not far away 'above the bright blue sky' but in a subtle way interpenetrates the physical world while remaining invisible because it vibrates at a quicker rate. The soul awakens after death in a state of consciousness rather than a geographical location, and may well think it is in some familiar place

65

it loved on earth. The planes closest to earth seem so familiar and ordinary that people who 'die' suddenly or unexpectedly often have no idea they are dead and only gradually come to understand their new state. They have bodies which are an exact counterpart of the physical and can enjoy life as they did before, but with subtle differences. For instance, a thought becomes much more quickly manifest. On earth it takes some time for a conception to materialise, whether it is a conscious idea that has to be brought into actuality with effort and determination, or the unconscious thoughts that gradually stamp themselves in the lines of the face and the set of the body. In the planes beyond death, however, matter is not so dense, and is therefore more quickly moulded by thought.

The planes closest to the physical are known as the astral planes. They range from a dark and sordid replica of coarsest and crudest earth-conditions to places of breathtaking beauty, where wonderful scenery, gracious buildings, homes, schools, universities and temples of wisdom are to be found. These higher astral planes are often known as 'the summerlands' because the conditions there are always summer-like.

The soul awakens to surroundings which reflect its habitual thought-life. If the thought-life has been stormy or bitter, the conditions in the astral world will closely reflect it. If, on the other hand, the man habitually delights in all that is kind and true and beautiful, then he awakens to a world rich in beauty, an externalisation of his own thought.

These astral planes, although often very beautiful, are only the beginning of the journey. The soul may remain there enjoying a normal and familiar life, full of interest and with plenty of scope for expressing natural gifts and inclinations, for a long or short period; but at some point it will feel the urge to seek deeper understanding. It will see a light on the distant mountains and be drawn towards it. Thus it will be led onward into the higher mental and later the celestial planes of being, from which it can review the whole picture of its past lives, and be shown the grand panorama of the soul's evolution.

After a period of complete refreshment and recharging in the heaven world, the time comes for the soul to reincarnate for another period of experience. When the moment of departure comes there may be as much of a wrench as there is at the end of a life on earth. However, as the soul grows in wisdom the difference between 'here' and 'hereafter' becomes less marked and much closer communion between the two worlds exists. We are told by White Eagle that as the influence of the Aquarian Age increases, more advanced souls are coming into incarnation, to whom the veil between the two worlds will be almost transparent. In the future every man will learn how to build his own bridge between the worlds so that he can receive inspiration, consolation and strength therefrom. One of the basic tenets of White Eagle's teaching is that we must learn to rely, not on a medium or on any outside source, but on our own inmost spirit when we seek communion with those in the next world.

6. Finding the Inner Light

As we have seen, the physical body and conscious mind are by no means the real self, but only its outer manifestations. The capricious impulses and desires which spring from these are the least reliable guides to harmonious living. They are as a magnet which holds us firmly to earth, and unless we make the mental and spiritual effort to overcome this gravitational pull we shall be hopelessly bogged down in materiality, and miss the opportunity which life brings for the spirit to gain strength. The whole purpose of incarnation is that the spirit, by constant wrestling with earthly problems, may learn to transform the dense earth-particles so that they are made more subtle and irradiated with light.

As we have seen, spirit is the flame of the living God within the human heart, whereby man is a child of God, 'made in his own image'.

Spirit is invisible and intangible. To come to grips with matter it must take form, or clothe

69

itself in matter; in other words, it must individualise. The first layer of its individuality is the soul, and the outermost covering is the physical body, by which spirit learns to govern and control matter. Perhaps the best analogy is a flower bulb, in which the coarse outer skin may be likened to the physical plane, and the inner layers to the various finer bodies, all of which clothe the flame of the spirit, or the perfect flower in embryo, within the centre.

Our five physical senses are the means whereby spirit learns to understand and manipulate matter in its crudest, most obdurate form. The greatest problem for man encased in the physical body is how to counteract the magnetic pull of earth and earthly concerns, which can render him insensible to the truths of his being and lead him to believe that the physical sense-life is everything. This in turn leads to the 'eat, drink and be merry for tomorrow we die' attitude to life. By this a great deal of unhappy karma is made, not because sensual enjoyment is wrong, far from it, but because such desires and impulses, when blindly indulged, bring suffering to ourselves and to other people, for which we must ultimately pay in kind.

How then are we to cope with this problem?

It has been said that God never leaves man

without a witness: a witness, that is, to truth and the source of truth. This is so both in an individual and a universal sense. No child is born without the inner flame, that spark of Christ, which is man's claim to immortality when he can establish it. No matter how humble the soul, no matter to what depraved circumstances it has been drawn by its karma, there lies deep in the heart an inner light which will urge the noblest action of which that soul is capable. That prompting of the spirit is deeply personal. Nobody has a right to interfere with one who is obeying this subtle prompting, for only the inmost spirit knows the path the soul must tread, if it is to gain the necessary experience and work out karmic debts. It is all too easy for outsiders to give advice, as Mr Worldly Wiseman did to Christian in *Pilgrim's Progress*; but it may easily draw the soul from its true course and create fresh difficulties. Every soul must work out its own destiny. It is 'saved' not by the vicarious atonement of one man, but by the promptings of the inner Christ. No greater service can be given to another than to encourage him to find and follow his own inner light, and the greatest service parents and teachers can give to young children is to help them to discover and live by this light.

In the pressures of modern life it is not easy for people to give time even to search their own inner feelings, let alone to look where conscience would lead them. The conflicting demands of modern psychological concepts, orthodox religious beliefs, and a rapidly developing science, leave the average person in a maze of uncertainty as to what *is* the right way to act, or what to believe.

To find the inner light, the only true guide through the maze of knowledge and argument which surrounds modern man, requires a daily discipline which few are prepared to impose on themselves. It means giving up time to quiet meditation and contemplation. It means withdrawing from the daily clamour, retiring into the sanctuary of one's inmost being, and by an effort of will and aspiration stilling all the thoughts and desires of the outer world. This is perhaps most easily done in a church or dedicated sanctuary, or in some quiet place away from the conflicts of human life. It is not always possible to escape to such a place, or indeed to find it, except in imagination; nevertheless, an effort should be made each day to be alone and quiet. This done, firmly relinquish all cares and problems by consciously relaxing your body, stilling the senses, and with an effort of will direct your thoughts to some place or object which is for you the epitome of beauty and peace. Use all your creative imagination to visualise it. Suppose, for instance, that you choose some lonely seashore. First create in your mind the atmosphere; the light and movement of the sea, the strength of the deep-running tide, the peace of the far horizon. Hear the sound of the waves breaking on the shore, the cry of the sea-birds; smell for yourself the tang of the seaweed, and see the infinite variety of colour and shapes in wet pebbles and shells. Create, create, create! Build the scene clearly in your imagination, then hold the picture while you drink in the peace and strength which is also the source of your being, the source of all beauty.

For some, the scene which brings most help will be a mountain panorama, a quiet woodland by running water, or a sunlit flower garden. Others may choose a church or sanctuary, or even a perfect flower such as a rose or water lily. Create in your mind whatever form of beauty brings you personally the keenest sense of joy and healing, and draw from it the peace and strength you need.

Why should this practice of creative imagination help in coping with life's problems? Certainly it helps the higher self to escape from the imprisonment of the flesh and the lower mind, but it does more than this. When the soul is immersed in the problems of the outer life, it is cut off from its source of strength and guidance; but deliberate retirement from the conflict at regular intervals renews and strengthens the line of light with the true self, the spirit. Merely to sit quietly without thought-control and direction, merely to pray in the orthodox manner, so often ends in milling round mentally and emotionally on the same old problems; but when by an effort of will and concentration we direct our thoughts to a different level, we begin to build the bridge to the inner worlds, across which angels of light can come to minister to us.

Some people advocate making the mind a complete blank, but White Eagle does not recommend this; it is too negative and opens the consciousness to psychic and elemental forces which might be mischievous. There is so much yet to be learnt about the inner or higher worlds, and about human consciousness, that the only safe way to meditate if you are a beginner is first to create some image of positive beauty that will itself lead you inwards and upwards and, as it were, protect you, until you can make contact with and receive guidance from your own inner light. For surely, surely, this guidance *will* come. It will take time, patience and self-discipline for true contact to be made; but if you persevere in creating a sanctuary of beauty in your own mind, you will find that your course will gradually become clear to you. You will know from your inmost self what you must do. When this conviction comes, follow it at all costs; your own light will lead you unerringly to find true happiness and fulfilment. When you are in doubt or perplexity, bombarded with good advice from all sides, never take action until within your own secret sanctuary you receive this guidance from your own 'Christ Star'. It will never fail you.

Another practical way of strengthening the 'line of light' between the greater, eternal self and the limited consciousness of everyday life is through controlled deep breathing.

Even from a purely physical point of view, the practice of deep breathing is valuable, in that it cleanses and revitalises the bloodstream through the myriad tiny capillaries in the lungs. But more than this, breath, air, is closely linked with the thought process and gentle, deep breathing can be the first step towards bringing peace to the troubled mind. Moreover, by mental and spiritual attunement we can increase our intake of the divine life force, known in the East as prana, which renews the whole bloodstream. A tremendous hidden power is here available to all who will take the trouble to find and use it.

First of all, what is meant by 'deep breathing'? Students of hatha yoga, and students of singing and voice production, will understand the physical technique of diaphragmatic breathing, or the full yoga breath. For those who have not yet studied this technique we will go through it as clearly as possible.

Stand or sit comfortably poised, with the spine straight; or if preferred, lie flat on the floor and relax. Try to be near an open window, or in the fresh air, for your regular practice, but when breathing to calm your mind in times of emergency this is not essential. Now breathe out and out and out until every scrap of air is emptied from your lungs; and even then, try to let go a little more. This will make you contract your abdominal muscles as you push the last of the breath out. Pause a second or so, then consciously relax and let your abdominal muscles go; let the incoming air push the abdomen right out as the lower part of your lungs fills up; then *slightly* contract the abdomen and consciously feel the air flooding the middle part of your lungs, expanding the rib-cage to its full extent—but gently and in a relaxed way—then finally feel the air filling the top of your lungs. This may make you raise

76

your shoulders slightly, but keep relaxed, and don't fill the lungs to bursting point—there's plenty more air waiting for the next breath! Now hold the breath gently for a few seconds—not more than three to begin with, but when you are well in practice you can gradually increase this holding time—then gently breathe out and out and out as before.

This sounds a very simple process, so simple that it is hardly worth bothering about, yet it can become a key factor in transforming mind and body. If you are practising deep breathing for the first time, try to establish a rhythmic count for exhaling and inhaling, with two or three seconds pause between them. Your own pulse rate will give you a useful personal rhythm for counting. Be very careful not to strain in any way; find the rhythmic count which you can manage easily and in a relaxed way, and persist with this count for at least a month before adding an extra beat. Be careful not to jerk the breath with the beats but keep the flow absolutely smooth; and for the first week do not try more than four breaths at a time or you may feel dizzy. Do the exercise three times a day if you can manage it; but if not, at least on waking and before settling to sleep. As you become more practised you will find that you can easily take ten beats for each exhalation and inhalation, with five beats in between, and do not attempt to hurry this. Do everything easily and peacefully. It is the steady persistence which brings the results. In *Forever Young, Forever Healthy*, Indra Devi considers that sixty deep breaths daily, taken either in four periods of fifteen or in three periods of twenty, should be our aim if we would keep the bloodstream fully oxygenated and alive with maximum vitality. But this is an ideal which can only be reached after constant easy practice.

It must be emphasised that the breathing described is to be used as an exercise. Don't try to practise it all the time, though it will inevitably deepen and improve your normal breathing, and upgrade your general health. Having learnt and practised the physical technique, so that it becomes automatic, let us now combine it with controlled thought.

Try to become still in mind and slow down your normal breathing just a little. Now think of God; think of that beautiful light which is trying to manifest through the limited physical brain. Hold the thought of this light like a beautiful shining star until it becomes steady and real to your inner vision. Now start your deep breathing by breathing out and out and out; as you do so let go of all worry-thoughts, all fear,

all mental and emotional turmoil, all resentment, all confusion and pain. Breathe it right
out; pause for a moment, then open your
whole being to the shining star and begin to
inhale. As you do so, that light pours in
through the top of your head and into the
heart. The heart begins to glow and to radiate
the light, like a small sun. The blood, which is
physically being recharged with oxygen, is also
magically recharged with the vital force of the
spiritual sun. It flows all through the body
carrying new life and healing to every part.
See this happening. See the light carried to
every part of your being through the blood-
circulation; and with all the strength of the sun
in your heart, think or say the words, *I am the
resurrection and the life. Behold, I make all things
new.* See the life-force of God healing, renewing, restoring any 'dis-eased' or painful part.
As you hold the breath for the usual second or
two see all this happening, then once again
breathe out.

This combination of controlled breathing
and controlled thought, when regularly practised, can work miracles. It is a way of bringing into operation the immense power of the
subconscious mind, which can be used to re-
create a sick body, to restore a troubled mind,
to disperse tensions, pain and congestion, and

gradually to overcome troublesome habits and addictions. The subconscious mind is far more powerful than most people realise, and far more absorptive. Like a sponge it sucks up all the impressions coming to it from the outside world, from the daily press, from human contacts. These impressions combine with the hidden thoughts, emotional reactions and karmic memories of the past, and exert an extraordinarily powerful effect on our physical bodies through the nervous system.

Socrates said that self-control is an exact science, but it is not a science in which the conscious will-power forces the self as an unwilling slave into uncongenial action. It is a science of feeding good, positive suggestion into the subconscious mind and letting it take over the task. This requires a certain steady effort and persistence; it requires understanding of our own reactions and needs; but it is a gentle, positive, effort, like diverting the energy and attention of a wilful, fractious child into paths of happy, creative activity.

As this God-breathing becomes habitual, you will automatically resort to it and find strength from it in any stressful situation. In the midst of the trials of daily life you will pause, become still in mind, and focus for a few seconds on that shining star above, at the same time breathing out the confusion and fear, and breathing in the light from above. Then the shining being by your side can direct a ray of light on to your problem so that when next you look at it it becomes clear. This works whatever the problem, be it physical, mental or emotional. The problems which beset us all need not pull us down, but can teach us to rise in spirit and to breathe in the breath of God which gives new heart, new courage, an upholding strength and a deep peace.

As the inner light grows stronger, the realisation dawns that the body is the temple of the spirit and that without a strong healthy body we cannot fully enjoy all the beauties of life on earth nor adequately use our own gifts in service to others. So part of the discipline of the spiritual path is to learn how to live harmoniously, eating wisely and taking sufficient time for relaxation and exercise in the fresh air and for sleep.

Most spiritual teachers advocate a vegetarian diet, both for improving physical health and for developing a keener awareness of the inner world of beauty which can be found in meditation. White Eagle, while not insisting that all his followers must immediately become vegetarians, holds this ideal before us. He tells us that by confining our diet to fruit and vegetables, grains, nuts and dairy produce we create a purer, more sensitive physical body, a better instrument for the spirit, the greater self, to use.

Quite apart from the cruelty involved in killing animals for meat, when we eat their flesh we absorb into our subtler bodies their feelings and instincts, especially their terror and anger at the time of slaughter, which strengthen all the animal reactions in our own nature and makes it more difficult for the shining spirit to master the lower self.

Of course there are parts of the world in which animal flesh or fish is the only diet available at certain times of the year; also many people who feel drawn to seek the spiritual path find themselves in circumstances or family environment which makes it extremely difficult for them to have a non-flesh diet.

White Eagle's teaching makes full allowances for such difficulties and does not advocate our creating problems for our companions by being rigid and fanatical in our attitudes, or by forcing the body suddenly onto a non-flesh diet. He teaches, as did Jesus, that what comes out of our mouths (i.e., kindly speech) is far more important than what goes in, but nevertheless he holds before us the ideal of a simple vegetarian diet, rich in fresh raw fruits, vegetables and whole-grain cereals and as free as possible from chemical additives.

82

7. Building the Etheric Bridge

When, in *Pilgrim's Progress*, Christiana enters the Interpreter's house through the wicket gate, she is shown a series of pictures to help her on her path. One of them is the Man with a Muck Rake, his eyes fixed on the ground, scrabbling in the mud. By his side stands a shining being, an angel who watches over him with tenderness; but the man with his eyes entirely on the ground remains unaware of the help he could receive.

A deep truth can be seen in this picture. Every soul on earth has a friend and teacher in the inner world whose task it is to give guidance, comfort and strength to his charge. Yet most people are so absorbed in worldly problems that they remain deaf and blind to such helpers. Your guide is one who has known you through many incarnations, so that there is a strong link of love between you. As you learn to seek and find the eternal beauty within your own hidden sanctuary, you will awaken and

83

become receptive to the help that your guide can give.

At first, the wisdom of the spiritual guide is not easy to distinguish from the voice of conscience, because it is through the inner light, the highest self, that you make the contact with him. But after a time you will learn to recognise the presence of an unseen helper and to know his companionship, which brings courage and solace in times of sorrow and difficulty and added joy when things go well.

It is not always easy to find the peace of our own inmost sanctuary, because we get caught up not only in our own emotions and thoughts but in those of our close associates, indeed of all humanity. This is especially true for those who live in cities, or closely-linked communities. The turmoil of the thought plane is incessant, and it takes a strong effort of will to see through this to 'the light on the hills'.

Communal worship is valuable here, for it can help us to break through the thought forms immediately surrounding the earth.

The Master Jesus said, *Where two or three are gathered together in my name, there am I in the midst of them.* What happens is that collective worship creates a strong, aspiring thought-form which, like a shaft of light, cuts through the turbulence of the lower astral and mental spheres. Like Jacob's ladder it reaches the higher worlds. Down this ladder come shining ones, angels and ministers of grace, and even our own friends who have left this life. According to the sincerity of our individual aspiration in collective worship, we not only create this 'ladder of light' more strongly for ourselves, but we assist others to do likewise. Unity of aspiration gives increased strength, for the combined power of the group is greater than that of all its members working alone.

The important point to remember is that the key of the door into the inner world is on our side of it, and until we turn the key those who would help us cannot come through the door.

White Eagle, throughout his ministry, which has gone on for fifty years, has always taught his followers that the only way to find heaven on earth is to keep on steadfastly practising positive loving thought and giving kindly service in one's own sphere. He teaches how regular quiet meditation and aspiration will strengthen that divine flame which shines through every soul, and how through soul-effort that flame can be projected as healing light to serve others who are in need. His teaching embodies the true spirit of the Aquarian Age in that he guides us to work together in groups, to combine that flame within our hearts and by our creative power to form it into a blazing six-pointed star whose light radiates into the world. This technique is not to be used for selfish ends, to gain beautiful mystical experience. It is a complete giving of the whole being in service to God and mankind, a conscious dedication to the work of radiating the Christ Star to bring peace, comfort and spiritual illumination to those in need. Through this work there comes a spiritual bondage, one healer with another, those still in a body of flesh combining in mystic union with those in the world of spirit, all dedicated servers of the Christ. It is a union bringing indescribable mystical experience day by day, year by year.

Every time such a group gathers to seek God and to radiate the light in service, a spiritual power is created in that spot, which lingers long after the participants have returned to their earthly duties. The constant spiritual work gradually creates on the etheric plane around and above the actual physical building a beautiful temple of light, a focal point for the angels of healing who gather and remain to bless all who enter the earthly sanctuary. Spiritual power thus generated is never lost. It permeates the very earth itself and remains to bless future generations with an indescribable fragrance which brings balm to weary souls.

By the Law of Correspondences, our earthly lives are closely linked with the movements of the sun and planets; and at certain times of the year, when the sun is at particular points of the circle of the zodiac, there is a special outpouring of spiritual light. Services of worship held at these times can bring a special blessing to the participants. The Christian Church celebrates several of its festivals at these times of power, having adapted for its purpose Mithraic sun-worship festivals which were observed ages before the birth of Jesus.

In ancient times four great solar festivals were observed, corresponding to the solstices (Christmas and Midsummer) and the equinoxes (Easter and Michaelmas). Recent scientific research confirms that sun-temples such as Stonehenge were oriented to counterpart the position of the sun or stars at certain times and seasons.

At the present, the only two festivals which are really observed in the Western world (and probably more in a commercial than a religious spirit) are the winter solstice—Christmas, celebrating the 'rebirth' of the sun, the point at which it begins to return after reaching its most Southerly declination from the equator; and Easter—the ancient festival of the spring equinox (corresponding to the Jewish Passover) in which the people of the Northern hemisphere rejoice in the resurrection of life all over the earth.

All these physical phenomena have a spiritual counterpart, and as the light of the inner life grows stronger in the New Age, man will gain greater strength and clearer vision from these outpourings of spiritual power.

Special help is afforded to those who are bereaved, if they will avail themselves of it, when the sun is passing through the sign of Scorpio. The orthodox Christian festivals of All Souls and All Saints are held at this time; and, since more recently, the festival of Remembrance. Scorpio is the sign connected with death and the afterlife, and while the sun is passing through it the psychic power is such that the veil between heaven and earth is lifted. At such time, those in the land of light can draw especially close; it is as if the thought-fog surrounding the earth is thinned by the strength of the spiritual sun, and in a Remembrance Day service, with its atmosphere of love and devotion, a particularly strong bridge is built, which makes communion possible between those still on earth and their companions in the world of spirit.

The celebration of holy communion in the church is based on ancient Mithraic ceremonies of a similar nature. In the New Age, when the significance of the bread and wine is better understood, these outer symbols will not be necessary, for the true holy communion is made in a man's heart. When he learns to seek his own inner light, that light which is part of the Christ Spirit, his 'Christ star', he will find mystically that his own small light is one with the whole, a small flame within the unimaginable glory of the spiritual Sun. And from this spiritual Sun he draws sustenance and strength.

Once the secret of this inward communion is discovered, the whole of life is changed. The man who has found the Source of light, sometimes known as the mystical Holy Grail, becomes radiant, and healing spontaneously flows from him to his companions, according to their need. They may not regard him as good or pious in the accepted sense, but they will respond to the warmth and light which comforts and encourages them in their own struggles.

8. Original Sin

The old doctrine that all men are born in sin, and can only be saved by the redeeming blood of Jesus, is a distorted version of the truth that every soul comes into incarnation with certain karmic debts to be discharged during the earth life, and with certain traits of character to develop or to transmute so that they manifest positively rather than negatively. Karma can only be fully expunged through earth experience, and the courage and patience needed for this springs from the inner light, the Christ within the heart, which is man's 'saving grace'.

As well as all the suffering caused by religious fanaticism and bigotry during the Piscean Age, the doctrine of original sin has left a deep scar on many souls in the Western world. The idea that man is born in sin has caused many sincere people to be tortured by guilt, especially over sex. Even today, when such doctrines are fast losing ground, this subconscious guilt-complex often persists, causing widespread unhappiness.

Sex force is fundamentally divine fire or

energy which man must learn to govern and use both for the creation of new bodies in the world, for moulding material substances into beauty and usefulness, and for the destruction of what has fulfilled its purpose. Just as electricity has positive and negative poles which must balance each other, so the sex force in man is both creative and destructive, and it must ultimately be brought under the control and direction of divine will. As man evolves he will gain increasing control over this divine creative fire in himself. He will be able to use it not only in creating new bodies for souls coming into incarnation, but also indirectly for renewing and beautifying the earth itself. The creative fire of sex is the hidden energy behind all noble and artistic achievement, all humanitarian enterprise, and all feats of human endurance. Religious mystics know that the mastery of this force gives them occult power which can be used either for healing or destruction.

This was most wonderfully demonstrated by the great Indian mystic Gandhi, who started adult life as a simple government official in India. He came to England to gain his legal qualifications and in so doing broke the laws of his caste, so that he was rejected as an outcast. During the course of his legal work he was sent to South Africa, and there became more and more distressed at the treatment meted out to his people by the petty officials of the white European government. Gradually he became fired with the realisation that he must do everything within his power to help his beloved countrymen to realise the dignity of their age-old culture and to fight for their human rights. Although Gandhi did not allow himself to become attached to any orthodox faith (he loved the Sermon on the Mount quite as much as the Bhagavad Gita), he was deeply religious. He knew that violence of any kind was wrong, but he also understood the tremendous power hidden within a man's soul which would enable him to stand up to the greatest possible odds and to lead others towards the attainment of an ideal. He well knew that this soul force (satyagraha) is associated with the sex fire, and could be greatly strengthened and intensified through living a celibate life. Therefore, before embarking on his African campaign of passive resistance, with the full and willing consent of his wife, he took a vow of celibacy which he kept to the end of his days. He never forced this path upon anyone else, but his closest followers and helpers took the same vow. The story of Gandhi's life, the record of his work in Africa and later his miraculous achievements in India help one to realise the immense soul power which can be generated and used in service by a man who has fully learnt how to control and redirect the sex energy. In Gandhi's case, it roused a great nation from its lethargy, and freed his beloved India from foreign domination.

It is for the same reason that in the beginning the Church insisted on a celibate priesthood. The Age of Pisces was a period when the souls of men needed such occult power to manifest in a church which could hold them through simple faith and help them to touch inner and inexpressible mysteries in divine communion. This communion is symbolised in the fish, swimming in the ocean of universal life and absorbing nourishment from it. With the approach of the Aquarian Age the stimulation of the mind has tended to destroy the mystical aspect of religion, for during this age the mind, as well as the emotions, must be satisfied. Nevertheless the need to govern and channel the sex force is as imperative today as it was yesterday and is always.

With the removal of so many religious and social taboos, young people today are exposed to much greater stresses through the stimulation of sex fire than in the past. There is an immense commercial exploitation of sex awareness, in advertising, in the press, in films, plays, books, and on television, all of which acts like the Whore of Babylon in over-stimulating the desire-nature.

Although in these enlightened days it is customary to discuss sex problems freely, this too may not be entirely helpful. According to the Ancient Wisdom the creative sex fire is a secret, sacred thing. In astrology it comes under Scorpio, the sign of secrets, of hidden inner power. All the exploitation of sex and free discussion about it, while it has been a necessary antidote to Victorian prudery and Piscean misconceptions, nevertheless dissipates much of its magical power and beauty. You cannot experience the full joy of a rose by pulling it to pieces, petal by petal. There is in the whole flower an indefinable magic and fragrance which is destroyed by dissection. Yet real knowledge is necessary and helpful, not only knowledge of simple biological facts, but also an understanding of the significance of sex.

The age-old law of sex is rather beautifully demonstrated in astrology by the fact that Mars, the planet of divine fire and energy and the planet which rules the generative centre in man, is 'exalted' (at its best) in the sign of Capricorn, the sign of family responsibility, ruled by Saturn. This clearly indicates that sexual union should only take place with each partner accepting full responsibility for the happiness and well-being of the other and to provide a secure happy family life for any children of the union. Saturn in turn is exalted in Libra, the sign of partnership and marriage, the sign of beauty, balance, harmony and happiness ruled by Venus. There is no doubt that the blessing of sweet human happiness comes to man perhaps more through happy family life than in any other way.

Astrology tells us that India comes under the sign of Capricorn and it is interesting that the people of that country are brought up with a deep understanding of the beauty and the power of the sex force. People are inclined to think of all Indian yogis as ascetics, but this is by no means the whole picture. It is recognised and fully understood that the powerful sex energy is not limited to purely physical expression. It is a spiritual fire which can be channelled, trained and transmuted to bring to man's soul the most wonderful expansion of consciousness where the individual loses all sense of separateness and experiences the indescribable joy of union with the divine power, the source of all being. This indescribable experience is the goal of all yoga training, whereby the divine fire and energy hidden in the generative centre of man and known as

95

kundalini, is gradually raised from the purely physical outlet, through creative expression in the emotions, through creative mental expression, to expression on a higher mental plane and finally onto the celestial plane of heavenly illumination. This process of transmutation and channelling of the divine fire requires a long, slow process of aspiration and training.

The purely physical expression of this force is however extremely important, for while man is bound by karma to the wheel of rebirth, fresh bodies must continually be provided for incoming souls. This again is well understood in India where the young people are trained from childhood to understand and appreciate the importance of a happy sex life. The boys especially are trained in the art of happy sexual union. Marriages used to be arranged at a very early age, the partners being chosen according to the mutual blending of their horoscopes. The importance of the discipline of family life, and of accepting family responsibilities was understood.

Gandhi was very much against such child marriages, although he himself was married at the age of thirteen to a girl of his own age and she was a devoted wife to him, helping and encouraging him in every way possible in his great mission. One cannot help wondering whether these child marriages, arranged with due care according to the harmonious blending of the horoscopes and within a strong supporting family framework were not just as sensible an arrangement as our Western method of providing the Pill for schoolgirls!

In marriage the sex fire finds normal healthy outlet, which ideally should bring joy and contentment to both partners, thus creating a secure and happy environment for the children. The individual needs of men and women vary so greatly that usually the process of mutual adjustment sexually, as in other ways, takes wisdom, patience, and a sense of humour which enables the partners to see minor difficulties in their true proportion. Where each is sincerely anxious to give happiness, and to fulfil the needs of the other, there will be rich blessing on the union.

Some conscientious Christians, steeped in the Piscean conception of celibacy as the ideal and holy state, believe that while the sex act is a biological necessity for the continuance of the race, it should be reserved only for the procreation of children. This idea limits to a purely animal level a function which, rightly understood, can lead human beings to an awareness of divine mysteries. Sexual union, when consecrated by true love and self-giving, can lead to a mystical comprehension of that divine union of the soul with the Cosmic Christ, a soul experience of indescribable beauty and joy. True love is infinitely more than a physical urge. It is the mature result of shared experience, and all the disciplinary responsibilities that the marriage partnership brings. This is why the idea of a 'trial marriage'—as though sexual union were all of marriage—has a touch of the ridiculous, for there can be no such thing. Only on the basis of the emotional security which marriage vows should bring can the true soul union, the joy of a good marriage, be established. Whether such vows are made in church or registry office or whether they are taken privately in the heart does not matter. They are binding according to spiritual law and cannot lightly be disregarded.

If we study the cosmic cycle of man's evolution, symbolised in the signs of the zodiac, and taught in parables in the Christian bible, as well as in all the great world religions, we discover that in the beginning every child of God came forth in dual form. *Male and female created he them.* In other words the original, new-born child of God is androgynous, as the perfected soul will be; but (to put it very simply) at a certain point in their evolution the two halves separate, in order that each may gain fuller experience. This truth is shown in symbolic form in the story of Eve being fashioned from Adam's rib. To Adam and Eve alike is given the gift of creative energy, both positive and negative, but they are unaware of this power until they have eaten of the tree of knowledge of good and evil. *And the eyes of them both were opened, and they knew that they were naked.*

In other words they then became aware of themselves as individuals, living apart from each other, apart from God, possessing freewill to choose the path either of good or evil, god-likeness or selfishness. So, in the words of the biblical parable, *Unto Adam also and to his wife did the Lord God make coats of skins, and clothed them. And the Lord God said, Behold the man is become as one of us, to know good and evil.*

At this point in evolution the twin souls leave the protection of the Garden of Eden and become completely embodied in the flesh, with individual minds which must be trained and developed through experience in matter. The man and woman must now take separate paths in the physical life for many incarnations. This stage is usually called the fall of man, but the term is so linked with the doctrine of original sin and other misconceptions of Piscean ortho-

99

doxy that perhaps a better description would be the descent of man into the bondage of physical matter.

As each aspect of the twin soul begins to exercise the gift of freewill, the Law of Cause and Effect is set in motion. Through the resulting experiences of joy and pain, each evolves first to full individual consciousness, and then to an awareness of the needs of others. Slowly there dawns an understanding of the universal brotherhood of life which eventually leads the soul-twins to reunion, and through their selfless love to an expansion of the limited human consciousness into the divine, or Christ-consciousness, that wonderful union which is the end of all our striving.

The separation of twin souls is a vital aspect of evolution. Were they allowed to stay together, wrapped up in each other, they would feel no urge to progress. It is the deep, unconscious yearning of each of the twins to be reunited in true love that gives every man and woman, immersed in physical matter, a longing for a beauty not of the earth, and an urge to seek truth. Each separate entity must come to earth countless times, sometimes in a male, sometimes in a female body, though always retaining its fundamentally active or passive aspect of creative energy, in order to realise to the full the joyous, creative potential of man and woman living and working together in the light.

Although soul-twins rarely come together in marriage until a certain point in the evolutionary cycle, they may incarnate in other family relationships. Again, they may not necessarily incarnate at the same time. If one remains discarnate while the other takes a body of flesh, because the link between the two is so strong and bright, the one in spirit can help and inspire the other working on earth.

White Eagle teaches that humanity as a whole has now passed the lowest point of its evolutionary cycle and is advancing towards another age of harmony when the whole earth will become more etherealised and beautiful. The time is approaching when twin souls will more frequently be allowed the joy of working together in human marriage, their lives devoted to the service of humanity, so that their united love becomes a beacon flame to warm and inspire all within their environment.

The new Age of Aquarius will bring an ever deeper understanding of the meaning of brotherhood between men and nations, and as more advanced souls come into incarnation more marriages of this kind will bless humanity and speed up the evolution of the whole race.

The more advanced the soul that descends into incarnation as a child, the greater its need for a deep and true love between its parents. Soul-twins drawn together in marriage can reach a degree of harmony and understanding which at times raises human love to an almost divine level, and through this a pure and lovely body is created for the incarnating child. Such love creates light; it engenders conditions in the home and family life which will enable the child to grow strong in spirit.

Karma in marriage and family life need not necessarily be brought over from a past incarnation. By our present thoughts and actions we continually make fresh karma, either good or bad. Ungoverned emotion, careless destructive thought and speech, always sets in motion a train of karmic reactions which may take many incarnations to work through, thus delaying for an indefinite period the soul's progress towards complete happiness and freedom. On the other hand, every effort towards self-control, consideration and kindness within family relationships makes good, positive karma which not only speeds up the progress of the individual soul but helps many others on the upward climb.

The fact that marriage between twin souls is rare in no way implies that the average marriage cannot bring a couple deep happiness. The whole plan of evolution depends upon the provision of new bodies for incarnating souls, and the creation of a happy, healthy family is a service to life, which brings its own rewards. Normally, souls are drawn together in marriage to work out, each with the other, karma which can only be discharged in this way. The marriage may then be used to provide suitable bodies for incoming souls who also have karmic links with either or both partners.

Men and women may also marry in order to accomplish some special work begun in the past and which they plan to continue in the future. Or, through the special quality of their loving friendship, they provide the right conditions for an advanced soul to incarnate. Such unions of old friends and comrades can be extremely happy. Children of these marriages, blessed with such a harmonious home life, are well-equipped for their own particular service in the world.

Like birth and death, marriage is controlled by karmic law beyond the scope of the conscious mind. Often the power which draws a couple into partnership is irresistible and quite beyond their personal volition. At the appointed time those who have karma to be worked out in marriage will be drawn together, perhaps through a series of apparent coincidences, even though they come from opposite ends of the earth. Similarly, if karmic lessons have to be learned through separation the same irresistible force will bring about the physical parting of those who truly love. Neither can religious vows of chastity be lightly broken, for when a soul gives a solemn pledge to God, for the sake of its own integrity it feels a deep need at some time to fulfil that pledge, again in the face of strong temptation. Or it may be drawn into a condition of environment or health which forces it into a celibate life. According to some of Edgar Cayce's readings, this breaking of a religious vow may sometimes be the deep underlying cause of such problems as frigidity or sexual impotence.

Although much is done in schools nowadays to teach children the biological facts of sex, our young people are much less protected from the exploitation of sex than ever before. Coeducation is undoubtedly good and healthy but it is difficult for young people to realise the tremendous natural force they are up against.

The greatest help is of course a secure and happy family life and parents who are truly loving to each other and their families. Sex attitudes are absorbed even during babyhood. Growing children almost instinctively feel and know about their parents' attitude to each other. Modern intellectual attitudes, the growth of women's lib, and the breaking down of the old secure family and religious background in so many cases, leave our young people ignorant and defenceless, filled with unrealistic ideas of romantic love. Many of them follow the attitude that they should 'have sex' whenever they feel like it and such are the pressures in society that often girls feel obliged to 'give in' to their boyfriends in order to keep them, or to be able to boast to other girls. All this is sad, for it degrades to a purely animal level a function which when properly understood can be a source of much comfort and consolation among the pressures of life; and when it is transmuted it can be a driving force which creates beauty, harmony, joy—a heavenly radiation blessing many souls.

White Eagle, in company with all spiritual teachers, tells us that the sex urge should only find physical expression in a dedicated partnership where each takes full responsibility for the happiness and well-being of the other. There is no place for promiscuity, or wife-swapping, or sex outside such a dedicated partnership. Responsibility is the keyword.

Only when all responsibilities have been fully and willingly discharged are the man and

105

woman free from karmic debt. This does not mean that divorce is necessarily wrong. There may come a time when each partner has discharged his/her debts and needs to go on to fresh experience—in which case the partnership dissolves almost naturally and without bitterness—but unless this is so, those concerned will be drawn together again and again, and cannot spiritually be free. In many cases it may therefore be more sensible to carry the burden and discharge the debts and so win through more quickly to happiness and enlightenment. This is entirely a matter for the individual conscience. No mundane judge, no mundane court of law can ever decide the issue.

Sometimes when in a previous life one partner has gained considerable power over the other a strange, magnetic emotional tie is set up in which he or she feels completely dominated, and is forced to accept all kinds of bullying, mental or physical. In such cases it may well be that the down-trodden one has to find strength and courage to make a break, both for the sake of children or for his or her own self-respect. Often it is love for the children that gives him the will to fight. Divorce is obviously the course which will be beneficial for all concerned, but the suffering partner must clearly recognise the need for the break, and be determined to go forward bravely into a new life.

Responsible, kind fatherhood; loving, wise motherhood; sacred marriage vows leading to a happy united family life—these have been the ideals of great races and civilisations throughout the ages.

Women in the New Age will realise and accept the importance of their true function of motherhood, and learn once again to wield their magnetic and emotional power with wisdom and gentleness. Within them lies the ability to inspire and draw forth the noblest aspects of manhood in courage, chivalry and tenderness, and through these qualities to create a partnership which will find expression not only in a secure and happy family life, but also in public service.

Whether or not they marry and bear children, women have the essential task of mothering humanity, of binding wounds and giving sympathy, homely wisdom and practical kindness to those in need. For them the sex urge is closely linked with home-making. The Ancient Wisdom teaches that a woman's most noble and important function is mothering, first those in her care within the small circle of her home, and then in a wider circle in the outside world, until her love becomes ever more universal.

107

While the will or father aspect of God calls life into being, the mother aspect creates and nurtures form. This means that every true woman feels the urge to create a home and to mother those in need of care. In modern life this instinct is often stifled and overlaid by intellectual interests, especially if in a recent incarnation the soul has been a man. The fact remains that souls incarnating as women are meant to express as far as possible the principles of divine motherhood. The future of the human race is in the hands of the Great Mother, and earthly women are her instruments. With them lies the responsibility for the health and well-being of the children of the future. That is why in sex relationships the woman should set the standards. Her response to sex is usually slower, but much more deeply emotional than a man's. For a woman sexual union normally awakens deep feelings which are in effect a preparation for the natural completion of the act in motherhood. This is why sex outside marriage can so often be psychologically damaging to her, apart from the risk of bearing unwanted children. The development of the contraceptive pill has of course given to women greater freedom than ever before from the fear of unwanted pregnancy, and on the whole it is no longer considered wrong for girls and boys to live together without marrying. If they take due care there is little or no risk of conceiving children. This does not alter the fact that from the viewpoint of spiritual law, as soon as a man and woman live together, a mystical bond, a karmic bond, is created. Whether or not they have children, they have taken upon themselves the responsibilities of marriage and all that it entails.

Because marriage is so deeply karmic, because it involves the dedication of one's whole life to making another person happy and to creating a secure happy family background for the children yet unborn, it surely seems good to set forth on this path with a religious ceremony invoking God's help and blessing.

To people with spiritual knowledge the way in which the contraceptive pill alters and regulates the essential functions of the ductless glands is a source of anxiety. These glands are closely associated with the chakras, the centres of psychic energy in the body which are deeply significant in the soul life. It seems unwise to tamper with them just for the sake of irresponsible sense gratification.

In our present state of spiritual development and understanding, it seems sensible and right to use man's technical skill to limit families so that each child can receive the best care, but for reasons given above, the various mechanical methods of birth control are preferable to the pill.

There is so much still to be learned about the conception and birth of children. Why should it be that some couples try for many years and are not blessed with children, and babies come to others in spite of apparently safe methods of birth control? Healthy babies just do not seem to be born to order however much man thinks he knows about it.

The reason is of course that children and parents are so closely linked by the laws of karma, through incarnation after incarnation—which is the true meaning of the biblical saying *the sins of the father shall be visited upon the children.* There is no doubt that sexual union touches the deepest springs of man's being and is therefore a potent means both of creating and working out karma.

This brings us to the deeply emotional issue of abortion, which is not really such a modern issue, for means of abortion have been sought by desperate girls throughout the ages, often with tragic results. Indeed the modern response to the problem, whereby abortion under proper medical care is freely available, is infinitely preferable to the terrible backroom experiments of the past. Deeply and instinctively most women feel that there is something wrong in abortion. As soon as a child is conceived, no matter in what difficult circumstances, there is an instinctive emotional reaction, deep and primitive, to guard and protect that life. When the surrounding circumstances are difficult or tragic this will be overlaid by many other tortuous, conflicting thoughts and feelings which may lead the desperate girl to seek an abortion. But it reasserts itself. The more kindly, caring society of the coming Aquarian Age will deal much more compassionately with these human problems, and even in our own century, through the wonderful work of the Salvation Army and more recent organisations which help the single mother and her child, many deserted girls have been helped to have their babies in peace and to choose whether to keep or have them adopted. Both courses inevitably involve much emotional strain and anguish, for which at some time the father of the unwanted child will have to make amends. In a future life, perhaps in a woman's body, he will go through almost identical experience, and will also learn what it is like to be the unwanted child of such a union.

When the girl is forced by fear, by the pressure of those about her and through her own lack of understanding to resort to abortion, this

111

makes a deep mark on her soul memory. Deep down she knows that only God can give life, that it is a precious gift from God. This gift, so lightly regarded, may in some future life be withheld, and the mother long in vain for the gift of children. This is the experience she has taken upon herself to clear the memory from the past.

Abortion that is absolutely necessary for the mother's health and the well-being of the rest of the family is quite another question, one of wise discrimination and responsible choice on the part of the parents. The sad decision is taken in love and sorrow, and full responsibility accepted for the well-being of others. Such a selfless attitude brings its own blessing for in soul karma, strangely enough, the deed is nothing and the motive, and memory of it, all. Truly loving, caring action is always blessed. Selfish action taken for the sake of convenience and sense-gratification can make heavy karma for incarnations ahead.

Control of the sex fire naturally presents problems to many young people before they marry and to those who for some karmic reason are denied the outlet of happy marriage. Even so if this is viewed in perspective and in relation to life's total activity, the problem should not assume unmanageable proportions. It does not hurt anyone to strive to control and redirect the sex fire. If karma denies a normal physical outlet in marriage, it means that here is an opportunity to learn how to control and use the creative fire in some form of active service or in the creation of beauty. All the energy of mind and body should be directed to making the world in some way a better and more beautiful place. Used in service, the sex energy can bring deep happiness to the soul, happiness which can be even more satisfying than purely physical gratification.

In yoga the control of the sex fire is well understood and there are certain exercises, particularly a simple breathing exercise, which can be very helpful to those with lack of an adequate outlet for the sex energies. It is fully described by Indra Devi in her book. 'First you must relax completely for a few minutes. . . . Then sit up straight, keeping the neck and head very relaxed and start doing the deep rhythmic breathing exercise.* Having taken five or six (or more if you are not a beginner) breaths, close your eyes and try to visualise a great vital force operating within and outside of you. Concentrate your mind on it, keeping away any thoughts connected with sex. Now resume again the deep rhythmic breathing and

* Described in chapter 6.

do the following: each time you inhale, imagine that you draw the sex energy upwards from its centre, like a pump drawing up water from a well, and each time you exhale direct it to the solar plexus.* Or, if you prefer, direct it to the brain to be stored there. Keep on doing this exercise for a few minutes without interrupting the rhythm of your breath. If you haven't done any deep breathing before, stop this exercise as soon as you feel dizzy and resume it only after three or four hours. Simple as it may seem its practice is very effective. It is essential, of course, to do the deep breathing correctly and to be able to will strongly that the sex energies should rise upwards before being directed to the solar plexus. Thus, these creative energies are not wasted, like in the practice of self-gratification, but are conserved by the system and are transmuted into a finer force, adding magnetism, vitality and attraction to one's personality. This exercise is of benefit for both men and women. The best time to do it is when passions are aroused and the sex urge is felt, although it can also be done at any other time. The combined practices of this exercise, the yoga postures and breathings will not fail to produce soon the desired results,

* The solar plexus is the energy battery of the body, where surplus prana (life force) is stored.

especially if you watch your diet and cut out all drinks and foods which act as stimulants.'

Indra Devi lists among the foods which act as stimulants caviar, oysters, fish, venison, pork, celery, spiced pickles and highly seasoned dishes, alcohol, coffee, chocolate and other drinks which have a stimulating effect! Of course a basic essential is a clean, natural, objective attitude towards sex, respecting its true dignity and trying to understand how this wonderful force can be channelled and trained into a transforming power.

The problem of homosexuality is one which of recent years seems to have come into prominence. Again it has always been with us but hidden and suppressed in that aura of guilt and secrecy which has bedevilled sex-teaching throughout the Piscean Age. Of recent years so much has this problem been discussed that many young people are even afraid to enjoy friendship with those of their own sex, and others are quite unnecessarily tormented by the fear of homosexual tendencies when, as they grow through adolescence and early manhood or womanhood, they find their wakening emotional life centred on one of their own sex. Such mental torment is quite unnecessary, for more often than not this is just a natural emotional awakening which helps to bring matur-

115

ity to the character and prepares the soul for an even deeper and more satisfying partnership with a member of the opposite sex. True friendship is the basis of any good partnership. It is of the soul and spirit, above the limitations of physical sex and one of God's most precious gifts to man. As our capacity for friendship widens, we begin to comprehend the joyous vista ahead of humanity in a brotherhood wide as the world. As Shakespeare said, 'Let me not to the marriage of true minds Admit impediments'.

Really to understand the problem of homosexuality one must realise that during the course of many incarnations we come back in bodies of either sex according to the particular lesson our inmost self is learning, and the work that has to be done. After a number of lives, say in a man's body, it is not easy for a soul immediately to adapt to the new dimension of a woman's body, for there may well remain in the subconscious a habitual attraction to women which in the past was felt strongly through experience in a male body. This will take time to die away. Similarly a soul in a male body for the first time after several incarnations as a woman may feel a like attraction to other men. Or again a soul who has spent an incarnation in a confined community,

116

like a monastery or convent, may well feel happier and more at home with others of the same sex because of much work done together on the mental or soul plane. So much depends on a soul's past experience.

Because of nature's need to produce new bodies for incoming souls there is an instinct in many people which gives them a deeply emotional reaction to any deviation from the normal physical sex urge. This attitude, of course, relegates the sex force to the purely physical or animal expression. We have to remember always that it is a creative fire expressible on many levels. Like electricity, it has a positive and a negative pole, and in the course of its development every soul must learn to master both, until, when perfect balance is achieved, the whole being becomes illumined and transformed. A symbol of this perfect balance is the Caduceus, the magic rod of Hermes, god of wisdom—the wand which all will learn to wield.

As previously stated, the expression of this divine creative fire can only bring to the soul the joy and ecstasy which it was intended to do when it is directed by a sense of duty and responsibility, and used in service to life as a whole. The sex of the body the soul has chosen imposes certain natural duties and responsibilities upon it and gives it certain aptitudes for service. To fulfil these obligations may well be more difficult immediately after a change of sex between one incarnation and another, and more soul-effort will be required—but this is all part of the soul training which will eventually lead to complete mastery of both poles of being.

Once we can accept that this interchange of sexual roles will continue until we can function equally well and happily in a body of either sex, putting our whole heart into developing the qualities, fulfilling the responsibilities and revelling in the joys of either type of body, this creative fire will present fewer problems.

Its control and direction will always need soul-effort and discipline, but this must not be confused with repression. To deny this force within oneself, to bottle it up and fight it, inevitably leads to psychological problems which may explode into all kinds of cruelty and violence. It leads to wretched guilt-complexes or a mental arrogance which can bring misery to others. If karma denies the normal physical outlet for the creative sex fire, it must be consciously directed into creative service, either on the physical plane through vigorous practical work, sport, or a hobby which uses up all surplus energy, on the emotional plane, through helping suffering people in some way, or through one of the arts which gives a good emotional outlet, or through the mind—not only in deep thought and study, but consciously directing and using soul power for healing people, and situations, as Gandhi did.

It is notable how many great musicians and artists have been unable to cope with ordinary married life. All their energies were poured into their artistic expression, and what a gift they gave to the world! Once this divine fire is raised beyond the limitations of the physical body, sex becomes a soul force, a beautiful power quite beyond our earthly minds to comprehend. Did not Jesus say that in heaven there is neither marrying nor being given in marriage? On the soul plane everyone will eventually learn to express in their own unique way the creative power of God, using equally the positive and negative energies to bring beauty, harmony, heaven on earth.

To achieve a master's degree in any of the arts and sciences takes a long period of concentrated effort. There are bound to be many mistakes, many blotted copybooks on the way. Striving to attain a master's degree in the use of this divine, creative fire is a far longer path, a soul effort of many many lives, during which lesson after lesson is gradually mastered, but every soul is involved in this struggle.

Sexual rules and customs differ all over the world; what is accepted as right in our community may be sinful in another, but one basic law is constant. We should always treat the life force with respect, obeying the rules of our own particular community, and we must always behave to others as we would like them to behave to us in similar circumstances. We must try to imagine their feelings and act kindly—not foolishly—but with a sense of responsibility. When we fail, we must do our best to heal any suffering we may have caused, but never allow ourselves to be weighed down by a sense of guilt. This divine fire is a joyous thing, the source of all happiness, beauty and fun. We must learn to enjoy it on whatever plane we are functioning and help others to enjoy it. We must learn to become so filled with this joyous, creative energy that we radiate healing, serenity and happiness wherever we may be. And when eventually we gain our master's degree, when we have learned to balance exactly the pairs of opposites, we bestride the winged Bird of Life and rise unencumbered into the heavens—into glorious freedom and power.

9. The Healing of the Nations

The Ancient Wisdom has never been allowed to fade out of human knowledge, although in the darkest days of materialism, or what might be called the lowest arc of the evolutionary cycle, the light was very nearly smothered. It has been kept alive through the centuries by small groups of men and women who were usually forced to meet secretly, since their discovery could mean imprisonment, torture or even death. The Ancient Wisdom brings to mankind enlightenment and spiritual freedom which may deprive the entrenched powers in the state of their hold upon the people.

These secret groups have had many different names such as the Essenes, the Albigenses, the Knights of the Holy Grail and the Knights of the Rose-Cross. By their devotion they have kept the light burning. It was the work of the mediaeval brotherhoods to transmit light wherever possible, and to carry it wherever they went: the light of the hidden knowledge which brings healing and peace; the light of human kindness and love. Some brothers of these inner groups are once again in incarnation, while in the invisible worlds there is a large company of shining souls who are known as the 'Star Brotherhood' or the 'Shining Army'. Their leader, who has been working for the enlightenment of mankind throughout the dark centuries of the Piscean Age, has many names by which he has been known during his incarnations. Perhaps the name which gives the best picture at the present time of this great and noble personality is the Wise Knight. Having attained the degree of mastership, he is well able to function either in a body of flesh, or in subtler bodies invisible to the naked eye. He has signs and symbols by which he gives to his own band abundant and continual proof that his is the master mind behind the steady expansion of their work, which is to bring healing and enlightenment to humanity. In past centuries he often used the symbol of the candlestick bearing a lighted candle as his secret sign. This symbol was well suited to that period of darkness, but for the dawning Age of Aquarius, during which the light of spiritual knowledge is destined to free mankind from the bondage of materialism, he has given a new symbol, a blazing six-pointed star—not the Solomon's Seal which is the symbol of the Jewish community, but a living, silver star, blazing with light, an ancient symbol representing man made perfect in the light of the spirit.

It is interesting that from ancient times, one of the symbols of the constellation Aquarius has been the white eagle, and also that the white eagle symbolises a special ray of light, the ray of St John, which is now shining upon humanity with ever-increasing strength as we move forward into the Aquarian Age. The white eagle has strong white wings which carry it towards the sun. The work of that dear personality whom many people know and love as White Eagle is to help humanity use the wings of their spirit to lift them above earthiness into the very heart of the sun. As a beloved spirit guide, many people find him so close to their human problems, whereas Jesus or Buddha or Krishna are so great and wonderful, so far above them, that they feel they ought not to bother them with petty problems. White Eagle, they feel, is more on our level and able to tap for us immediate sources of practical help. Yet White Eagle always encourages us to try and understand more fully the teachings of the great ones, and to feel deep within us the ray of love and light which shines through them to

123

illuminate our pathway. He shows us how we can make a real contact with them through that same light within our own hearts.

The shining six-pointed star is the symbol of a universal brotherhood of light more ancient than the earth itself. With the coming of the Aquarian Age this brotherhood in the world of spirit is drawing ever closer to people on earth. As we go about our daily business few of us realise how new is the world of spirit, and how close are those who help and inspire. So often we are led to speak a word or do a small action which may help another, quite unconscious of its effect on that other person, or of the shining brother by our side who has prompted it.

White Eagle is showing us how to follow the Christ Star, calling us together to work in brotherhood on the physical plane, teaching us to work in groups, focusing our minds on the shining Star, and projecting the light which is generated by the group working together in true brotherly love, to heal and bless humanity. In teaching us thus how to work together in a brotherhood under that great Star of the New Age to help all humanity to respond to the light, White Eagle is helping us also to quicken the light within our own hearts, and so to develop the wings of our spirit.

White Eagle teaches us to do this by trying

to think of the Christ Star every third hour and to radiate its light into the world. He encourages us to be tolerant and forgiving of all the little human weaknesses we see in each other— because whenever people work together in a group there are bound to be personality differences. We all have our own ways of looking at things; all have sensitive feelings, strong opinions and personal prejudices which cause conflict. Sometimes in spiritual groups it is even more difficult because people expect much more of each other and of themselves and are easily disappointed. The quickening light within makes the soul more aspiring, anxious to do and be good. It also increases the sensitivity of the whole nervous system, and this, alas, often results in a greater proneness to irritability and hurt. This is especially so when a group of people are working together to project light and healing. By their very efforts they come under a beautiful ray of light from the world of spirit which sensitises their whole being. For a little while they live in a finer, purer, more peaceful state of consciousness. When they return into their everyday selves, they are not always prepared for the harshness of the earthly conditions. It takes a good deal of practice to enable the soul on the path of spiritual unfoldment to remain always steady,

125

calm and poised, with the higher self in full control. Hence the great need always for tolerance and forgiveness and for guarding speech.

The mortal mind of man is like a balance; it responds either to positive or negative thought, and perhaps our only freewill lies in what our response shall be. Every minute, every hour, every day we have the freewill to think truly or falsely, to react calmly, wisely and kindly or sharply and resentfully to the events of the day. As well as this, we live in a world of thought. Just as the atmosphere around us is full of invisible vibrations of light and sound, of which our conscious mind is unaware, but which can be registered electronically, so it is also permeated by thought—the thoughts of the people around us; the thoughts which are put forth in a never-ending stream by writers and speakers in newspapers and on television. This mass of confused thought is like a great tidal river battering at our consciousness, and it has two streams. In its light and positive aspect it creates and builds, and in its dark negative aspect it destroys and tears down. Inevitably the mind reacts to the one or the other, with a continual swaying of the balance between positive and negative thought.

Through regular periods of meditation and attunement to the inner light, the Christ power

126

in the heart will begin to take control of our thought world and use its immense power for good, for creating harmony in our own body and environment, and into an ever-widening circle of beauty and light.

Good thought begins not in the mind but in the heart. It grows from a heart that is entirely centred upon the light, the Christ Star.

Those who are trying to tune in to the Star at the magical hours of 3, 6, 9 and 12 can be greatly helped by the God-breathing described in chapter 6. This attunement need only take a minute, the time perhaps for three gentle deep breaths, but during this period the Star in the heart is strengthened. For that brief minute it is in shining control of all the myriad thoughts forever jostling into the mind. As well as radiating the healing light to those who are in need, this regular brief contact with the Star in the heart helps us to become more discriminating about the thoughts we allow to enter the mind, and gradually we realise our God-given power to control and direct those thoughts.

This we shall learn to do in the New Age. Aquarius is a fixed air sign which symbolises the focussing or harnessing of thought power. Its astrological ruler is Saturn, the planet of concentration, of contraction, of focussing thought. The sign of Leo, ruled by the Sun, is the polar opposite of Aquarius, and the perfect balance of the two signs symbolises the power of the Christ Sun within the heart of man controlling and irradiating his thought. This power in the heart, shining through the thought, can bring health, beauty and harmony to the physical body and the environment. By every effort we make to still the outer mind and attune ourselves to the Christ within, by every effort we make as we breathe in the breath of God, to rise on wings of light, we are building for the future. We are building the body of light, that eternal vehicle of the soul, so that it shines more steadily through the physical body, and shapes it into health and vitality. During the New Age man will gradually learn how, while still in a physical body, he can live also in the eternal world of light and peace, where dwell those he loves.

The Star Brotherhood on earth is a growing band of dedicated servers, both visible and invisible, who realise the ancient truth that in spirit, in love, there can be no separation. They do not recognise death as a barrier, but train themselves to regard it merely as an incident on the long path of progress towards that state of enlightened consciousness in which the beauty and perfection of the spirit gives mastery over all the physical atoms, and life on earth is made wholly beautiful.

The aims of the Star Brotherhood are simple and definite: to heal the sick in body, soul and mind; to remove from mankind all fear of death and separation, and to establish on the earth plane the spiritual brotherhood of life—the brotherhood which includes *all* life, human and angelic; the life of animals, birds, insects, flowers, the etheric creatures of the earth, air, fire and water elements—the grand universal brotherhood of all life.

The spirit of mankind is even now crying out for the light of the Ancient Wisdom, but the Star Brotherhood in the invisible worlds needs the co-operation of people living in the flesh to help them to carry forward the great work of healing and enlightenment. There is nothing dramatic about this work. Knowledge of the inner light is not readily given; it must be earned by quietly persevering in service, often unnoticed. Nevertheless those who truly seek become steadily, imperceptibly aware, not only of the power of their own inner light, but of an apparently magical power outside themselves which guides and leads them into ways of peace and joy.

This light in the heart becomes a focal point, attracting to the individual soul a greater power than it can fully realise. If the divine flame is constantly fed by self-giving in kindly service and healing, it grows and gradually illumines all the wayward physical atoms, until the whole body, the whole life, is healthy and radiant. This work, which will go on far into the future, is more important than any mundane activity, for it brings light and healing to the very soul of mankind. It hastens the coming of the long-prophesied Golden Age when men and women will live in harmony, in peace, to enjoy the wonders of a science and creative power devoted to man's well-being.

The Master Jesus said, *The harvest truly is great, but the labourers are few.* The call to labour, the call to seek the truths of the Ancient Wisdom by effort and self-discipline, the injunction to project light in healing and service, goes out with particular urgency to the young, the vigorous in body and mind. Such work will never interfere with any practical employment; it will enhance it. Those who find and draw strength from the light in their hearts become ever more human, kindly and practical. The true saint, the true mystic, is a gentle, kindly person, unusual more by his thoughtfulness for others and his fund of quiet merriment than by apparent holiness. The secret of his understanding, his thoughtfulness, his joy, lies in his heart.

'The Wise Knight' has given the following simple instruction to all those who would hasten the coming of the New Age.

'The brother of the Star should advance beyond the limitations of the earthly mind and body. He should strive to overcome all egotism and selfishness; to live simply and purely in body, soul and mind.

'The brother of the Star should endeavour to develop himself to such a degree spiritually that he is able to carry with him the power to make others happy; the power to heal those who are sick in mind and body. He should endeavour to develop within him the power to help his brother man to overcome all fear of death.

'Go to your tasks, brethren. Look not back, but keep your vision on that perfect, blazing, silver-white Star of the Christos, dawn star of a New Age, an Age of universal brotherhood, when the light of the Cosmic Christ within every man will transmute and glorify the whole earth.'

For further reading

White Eagle's teaching on the Ancient Wisdom is given in a number of books compiled or edited from his actual messages, and those most relevant to issues discussed in this book are given below. His specific commentary on the Gospel of St John and the book of Revelation is given in *The Living Word of St John* and in *The Christian Mysteries* (out of print) respectively.

On the subject of life after death, there is *The Return of Arthur Conan Doyle*, edited by Ivan Cooke; and also White Eagle's *Sunrise: a book of knowledge and comfort for the bereaved*. For spiritualist classics the reader is recommended to the books of Silver Birch, published by Psychic Press, and Helen Greaves' *Testimony of Light* (World Fellowship Press, for The Churches' Fellowship for Psychic and Spiritual Studies, 1969). Recent evidence for survival is given in *Life After Life* by Raymond A. Moody, Jr. (Corgi, 1975).

On reincarnation and karma, the most important books are those based on the Edgar Cayce readings, including Gina Cerminara's *Many Mansions* (William Sloane Associates, New York, 1950) and *The World Within* (William Sloane Associates, New York, 1957). The most recent evidence for reincarnation is in *More Lives than One?*, by Jeffrey Iverson (Souvenir Press, 1976). In *The Illumined Ones* Grace

132

Cooke gives her own memories of reincarnation in ancient Egypt and as an American Indian with White Eagle.

Joan Hodgson has herself written three books on astrology, *Wisdom in the Stars*, on the soul lessons of the twelve Sun-signs; *Astrology, the Sacred Science*, which is concerned with the great cycle of human evolution; and *Planetary Harmonies*, an astrological book of meditation. Vera Reid's *Towards Aquarius* (Rider, about 1940) is another important book about the great Ages of man. A basic case for astrology is made in *Astrologically Speaking* by Ingrid Lind, (Fowler, 1982).

White Eagle books which give the reader a greater understanding of how to live in harmony with spirit include *Spiritual Unfoldment* (two volumes) and *The Path of the Soul*, although all his books have this same purpose; also *Meditation* and *The New Mediumship* by Grace Cooke. Indra Devi's book, which contains the yoga exercises given in chapters 6 and 8, is *Forever Young, Forever Healthy* (A. Thomas, 1955). There are many good books on yoga, but the reader may begin with those by Richard Hittleman, or any recommended by the Yoga for Health Foundation, Ickwell Bury, Northill, Bedfordshire, from whom the books are obtainable. An introduction to the vegetarian way of life, advocated by White Eagle, is given in Rose Elliot's *Simply Delicious*.

Unless a publisher's name is given, the books mentioned are published by the White Eagle Publishing Trust.

133